Cooking Light

PRESSURE COOKING

MADE SIMPLE

Cooking Light

PRESSURE COOKING

MADE SIMPLE

Slow-Cooked Flavor in Half the Time

Oxmoor
House

Welcome

Like the idea of making comforting, slow-cooked foods in half (or less) of the traditional cooking time without sacrificing taste? For quick meals with simmered-all-day flavor, nothing beats a dish prepared in a pressure cooker. Perfect for hectic schedules, it's the only tool you'll need to transform fresh ingredients and lean cuts of meat into satisfying dishes within a fast-food time frame—just put the ingredients in the pot, set the timer (and the pressure), and go!

From fall-off-the bone shortribs to meaty stews, hearty bean dishes to savory grains, and even decadent cakes to puddings, *Cooking Light Pressure Cooking Made Simple* is serving up over 100 recipes—half of which can be prepared in 30 minutes or less. Most recipes require less than 15 minutes of prep time—the pressure cooker will do the rest of the work for you. Plus, for making spur-of-the-moment cooking a reality, we give plenty of advice for stocking your pantry, fridge, and freezer with staples for endless flavor combinations and meal options.

Jam-packed with helpful tips, techniques, and mouthwatering recipes, this book is more than just a cookbook. We'll guide you through every part of the process, from teaching you how to use this handy appliance to getting pressure-perfect results every time you use it!

The editors of *Cooking Light*

CONTENTS

PRESSURE COOKING POINTERS

HOME-COOKED FOOD IN A FAST-FOOD TIME FRAME

Picture this: It's 5 o'clock, and you're heading home after a long day. You're tired and you have a craving for a luscious, homemade stew, but you scoff at the thought of getting that on the table by dinnertime. As you drive with your onboard GPS keeping you company, you dream of a futuristic gizmo that could make a slow-cooked meal in minutes. Yet the answer is one of the oldest time-saving devices in the kitchen: the pressure cooker.

If that conjured up images of your grandmother's hissing pot and tomato sauce exploding on the ceiling, the first thing to know is that those days are gone. Modern pressure cookers are completely safe, easy to use, and turn out food that tastes slow-cooked in a fast-food time frame. Brisket that takes 3 hours in the oven can be made in half that time in a pressure cooker. Spanish Chickpea Soup takes 1½ hours rather than 2½ hours. That homemade stew you were dreaming of in the car—how about Beef Bourguignonne in 46 minutes?

A pressure cooker uses high temperatures rather than low, so instead of cooking food all day, you can cook it when you get home and still have braised-for-hours results. If planning ahead isn't your strong suit, a pressure cooker might be the answer you've been looking for. Or if you see lamb shanks at the store at 5pm and want them for dinner that night, you can do that in the pressure cooker. You can also prepare dishes such as delicate risotto, quinoa, and seafood, and quicker-cooking vegetables like carrots and kale. Anything you can braise, boil, or steam—even chocolate cheesecake—you can make in a pressure cooker.

There's a huge range of foods that cook faster and taste better in the pressure cooker, and this book zeroes in on the ones you'll want every day. The familiar and crave-worthy ones like hearty beef chili, hot-sweet pork ribs, and comforting pot roast—dishes your family and friends will love tonight, this weekend, and over the holidays. Every recipe is built on a selection of versatile pantry ingredients combined with key fresh ingredients so it can be prepared quickly and easily. This means you can have dinner on the table with fewer trips to the grocery store and less prep in the kitchen, even when inspiration strikes at the last minute. Speed plus versatility. That's what pressure cooking is all about.

COOKING UNDER PRESSURE

How Pressure Cooking Works

It's really simple: Food and liquid are placed in a pot which is then tightly sealed to prevent steam from escaping. This causes pressure to build under the lid and the temperature inside gets super-heated. Under that amount of pressure, the boiling point of liquid raises to 250°, whereas at sea level, the boiling point is 212°. So, food cooks at a higher temperature and thus cooks in half to one-third the normal time.

But quick results aren't the only benefit of pressure cooking: taste is a factor, too. The pressure essentially forces the flavor of each ingredient into the others, a magical alchemy that amplifies the savoriness of everything in the pot. Chefs often cite this as the reason they love this cooking utensil so much.

Early and Present Models

Pressure cookers have been around since the late 17th century, when a French physicist invented one to soften meat and other foods for easier digestion. Since then, the technology has evolved and pressure cookers are now in their third generation of development. The fiddly ones, with a single valve on the lid, were the first generation and used mostly in the mid-20th century. Next came redesigned stovetop models with multiple valves and safety devices that eliminated the risks of earlier models. Then came electric cookers that adjust the pressure automatically; with an electric model there's no need to check while the food is cooking.

Modern pressure cookers are easy to assemble and safe to use. Just look to the Europeans for reassurance (and recipe inspiration). They have been using pressure cookers all along because their factories were putting out new and improved models throughout the 20th century, whereas US factories stopped making pressure cookers during World War II to retool for military purposes. As a result, lots of post-war American homes had pre-war models that were out-of-date troublemakers—hence the exploding pots. In the 1980s, the second-generation stovetop pressure cookers appeared on the market, many of them imported, and people realized once again how wonderful pressure cooking can be. Today, you can choose from safe, high-quality pressure cookers in a range of styles and prices. Designs vary from brand to brand, and you should always read the instruction manual that comes with the one you have.

GET TO KNOW YOUR PRESSURE COOKER

Here are the basic components you'll find in every pressure cooker:

The Pot

Think Heavy: A heavy pot with a thick disk on the bottom (usually a bimetal construction clad with copper) offers maximum heat conductivity. This means food won't scorch while browning, and the pot will come to pressure more quickly and hold pressure more steadily. A low, wide pot with a larger surface area for browning means you don't have to cook in batches, thus speeding up prep time. A straight-sided pot is better than a flared one where food can scorch in the area that overhangs the flame. Aluminum pressure cookers are popular because they are lightweight and less expensive. Stainless steel ones can be more expensive, but are recommended because they are heavier and more durable.

The Lid

Tight is Right: The lid is where these essential features reside: the locking handle, the pressure indicator, and the gasket (at right). A dual-handle lid can make the pot easier to carry than one with a single handle, especially for 6-quart and larger sizes. Because the comfort of the handle and the ease of locking the lid are so important, shop where you can touch a display model and open and close the lid as you would at home. Look for the UL-listing symbol on the package; this ensures the lid cannot be opened while the pot is under pressure.

The Gasket

Sealed for Security: A rubber or silicone gasket (sealing ring) lines the inside of the lid and creates the seal that causes pressure to build. Because it plays such an essential role, treat your gasket with care: It should be cleaned carefully after each use and inspected again the next time to make sure it's not cracked, drying, or frayed.

The Pressure Indicator and Valves

See to it: Timing is essential in pressure cooking, so the pressure indicator on the lid should be easy to see, even from across the room. Look for one that pops up rather than one that is flush with the handle. The pressure regulator valve on the lid should be easy to operate and open with a simple touch. Again, if you can handle a display pot in the store, you can evaluate these features more easily. There are several other built-in release valves in the pot; most have a minimum of three that you don't see, part of a built-in safety system.

Other Tools

Get Steamy: Some models come with cooking racks, trivets, or baskets, which can be used for steaming vegetables or making recipes such as cheesecake.

BUYING A PRESSURE COOKER

There are two kinds of pressure cookers on the market today: stovetop and electric. Both share the parts described on pages 14–15, although the pot for an electric model is built in so you don't have a choice of materials. Choosing between an electric and a stovetop model is a matter of convenience and price.

Electric

An electric pressure cooker will do some of the thinking for you. Once you have assembled a recipe in the pot, set the pressure level and cook time, close the pot, and walk away. Once it comes to pressure, the timer will automatically start and later shut off so you don't have to be nearby during cooking. When shopping for an electric model, consider its size: You want one with a small footprint and, if you're planning to store it on the counter, make sure it isn't too tall to slide under an upper cabinet. (However, never release pressure while any pressure cooker is under a cabinet; the steam can damage the paint or lighting located there.) Be aware that because most electric models come with more bells and whistles, they also come with a much higher price tag.

Stovetop

With a stovetop pressure cooker, you need to stay nearby until pressure is reached, and then start a manual timer and check the pot for steady pressure a few times during cooking. However, a stovetop model is better for browning ingredients since you control the heat under the pot, and there's usually more surface area to work with than in an electric pot. You can also use the bottom of a stovetop model for things other than pressure cooking, such as boiling pasta, giving it the appeal of dual purpose. Finally, stovetop models are easier to store and are often less expensive.

Size

The question of what size pressure cooker you need also can influence your decision on which type to buy. There is a broader range of stovetop models, from small 4-quart pots (popular with vegetarians and those who cook beans and legumes a lot) to mid-sized 6- to 8-quart models to giant (and very specialized) 40-quart canning models. For everyday cooking for an average-sized family, your best bet is a 6-quart, which comes in either stovetop or electric. That's the size used for the recipes in this book.

ELECTRIC VERSUS STOVETOP

Whether you choose to purchase an electric or stovetop model should be a matter of personal preference and ultimately meet your cooking needs. Below are model differences you should consider before selecting one over the other.

	Electric	Stovetop
Cooking Pot	Cooking pot includes a liner pot that's made with a non-stick coating and is less durable	Does not include a liner pot; made of stainless steel or aluminum and is more durable
Food Removal	Liner does not have handles, which makes it tricky to pour from	Pot has handles, which makes it easier to pour from
Heat Regulation	Built-in heating element prevents control over heat	Requires use of stovetop burner for heat control, which makes regulating heat easier
Release Method	Must remove lid for quick release method	Allows for cooling under running water for quick release method

How to Adjust Recipes for an Electric Pressure Cooker

We tested all our recipes using a stovetop model. If you use an electric model, follow these tips:

1. For recipes that instruct you to reduce a liquid by simmering on the stovetop, like a sauce or soup that needs additional thickening, use the browning setting rather than the simmer setting. The browning setting will increase the heat for better liquid evaporation.

2. When a recipe needs only 10 to 15 minutes of cooking once it reaches the desired pressure, use your own timer rather than the built-in one. In some models the timer start will be delayed, causing the dish to cook under pressure longer and resulting in an overcooked dish.

3. Avoid using the keep-warm setting to prevent overcooking.

4. For a quick release, turn off pressure cooker and remove lid with the steam escaping away from you.

5. For a natural release, turn pressure cooker and allow the pressure to release naturally for 15 minutes.

PRESSURE COOKING 101

Follow these basic tips for easy pressure cooking:

1. Assemble or Brown the Food in the Pot

Ingredients such as onions, meat, and poultry add depth of flavor if browned before adding liquid; for recipes that do not call for this step, just layer the food in the pot in the order called for in the recipe.

2. Add Liquid

Water, broth, wine, or juice must be added in order for the pressure cooker to create steam; each recipe will indicate how much is needed, but also check your pressure cooker's manual to learn the minimum amount your model requires.

3. Lock on the Top

Check that the gasket is in place correctly, and then attach the top to the pot; most models will click into place when the handles are properly aligned.

4. Bring to Pressure

This step can take 5 minutes to 20 minutes or more, depending on the amount of food and liquid in the pot and the pressure level required; an indicator on the lid will show when pressure has been reached. At that point, the cooking time begins.

5. Adjust Pressure

Once pressure is reached, adjust the heat to maintain steady pressure; an electric model will do this automatically.

6. Release Pressure

There are three methods for releasing pressure: Natural Release, Quick Release, and Cold-Water Release under the sink (see page 20).

7. Finish the Dish

If needed, simmer the dish on the stovetop until it has reached its desired tenderness or consistency.

THREE WAYS TO RELEASE PRESSURE

There are three ways to release pressure after cooking is complete before you open the pot. When you do open it, tilt the lid away from your face, as there will be hot steam inside.

1. Natural Release:

The pot cools down on its own after the heat is turned off. This can take 10 to 15 minutes or longer, depending on the recipe, and food will continue to cook while pressure comes down. This method is recommended for foods that foam during cooking, such as rice and beans, so the valves don't get clogged as they could if the steam is released quickly.

2. Quick Release:

The valve on the lid is opened to release steam right away. This is used often for faster-cooking foods such as vegetables or when the pot needs to be opened partway through cooking to incorporate other ingredients, such as adding rice to a soup or stew.

3. Cold-Water Release (Sink Method):

This is the quickest method and can be used only with stovetop models. To do it, take the sealed pot to the sink and run cold water over the lid, being sure not to let it run into the valves; never submerge the hot pressure cooker in water.

PRESSURE COOKER DO'S & DON'TS

Familiarize yourself with this list of do's and don'ts for the best results.

Do's	Don'ts
Read the manual first	Use an old pressure cooker model; buy a new one
Wash the gasket, pot, and lid with warm soapy water	Put the pressure cooker lid in the dishwasher
Cut food into evenly sized pieces for consistent results	Oversalt food; adjust for this at the end
Check the gasket for cracks or drying every time you pressure cook	Overfill the pot with food or liquid
Drizzle oil over the top of liquid when cooking beans or grains to keep valves from clogging	Store the pressure cooker with the lid closed; rest the lid on top upside down so odors don't accumulate
Tilt the lid away from your face when opening the pot, as the steam inside is hot	Add fresh herbs at the end of cooking to preserve their flavor

PANTRY STAPLES

Use this list to stock up on the basics for easy pressure cooking. If you keep these items on hand, you'll be able to make most of the recipes in this book. Plus, you won't have to stop at the grocery store each night wondering what you can cook for dinner.

Oils, Vinegars, and Condiments

Canola or vegetable oil

Capers

Dry wine: red, white

Honey

Hot sauce

Ketchup

Mustards: Dijon, spicy brown,
    whole grain, yellow

Olive oil

Pasta sauce

Peanut oil

Tomato sauce

Salsa

Sesame oil

Soy sauce

Vinegars: apple cider, balsamic,
    red wine, sherry, white wine

Worcestershire sauce

Beans, Grains, Pastas, and More

Dried beans: black, black-eyed peas,
    navy, cannellini, kidney,

Couscous

Egg noodles

Fettuccine, penne, spaghetti

Corn and flour tortillas

Stone-cut grits

Barley

Farro

Oats

Rice

Canned Goods

Broth: beef, chicken, vegetable

Chopped green chiles

Diced tomatoes

Olives

Roasted red peppers

Tomatoes: diced, plain, seasoned

Baking Essentials

All-purpose flour
Baking powder
Baking soda
Brown sugar: light, dark
Cornstarch
Granulated sugar
Nuts
Powdered sugar
Self-rising flour
Semisweet chocolate
Unsweetened cocoa
Vanilla extract

Spices

Bay leaves
Black peppercorns
Chili powder
Curry powder
Dried basil
Dried oregano
Dried rosemary
Dried thyme
Dry mustard
Ground cinnamon
Ground cumin
Ground ginger
Ground nutmeg
Red pepper: crushed, ground
Seasoning blends: Asian, Cajun, Italian,
    Mediterranean, Mexican

Refrigerator

Bacon
Broccoli
Butter
Carrots
Cauliflower
Eggs
Parmesan cheese
Milk
Onion
Garlic
Refrigerated pesto
Sour cream
Yogurt

Freezer

Frozen beef: ground beef, chuck roast,
    sirloin top roast, brisket
Chicken: breast, thighs, whole chicken
Pork: shoulder, bone-in chops, tenderloin

EVERYDAY PRESSURE COOKING

Here's the secret about pressure cooking: Once you've done it one time, you'll wonder why you don't do it all the time. With the recipes in this book, you can. There's such a variety of flavors and ingredients, you'll find ideas for work nights, company nights, weekends, and holidays. There are first courses, main courses, side dishes, and desserts. Before you know it, you'll find this old-time appliance to be one of your best modern-day kitchen allies. Combine the ingenuity of a well-stocked pantry with a few trips to the market for fresh ingredients, and you really can pressure cook every day.

Check out these helpful features that make cooking with *Pressure Cooking Made Simple* even easier:

PRESSURE PERFECT TIP:
Foolproof tips that guarantee success in preparing specific recipes

SWAP IN A SNAP:
Clever suggestions for tailoring the recipes for your family's taste or for the ingredients you have on hand

5 MINUTE PREP!

10 MINUTE PREP!

QUICK PREP TIME ICONS:
Highlight prep times that are less than 15 minutes for at-a-glance searching

SATISFYING BEANS

BLACK BEAN SOUP
with Cilantro-Jalapeño Relish

The fresh relish kicks up the flavor of this classic soup. If you prefer a thicker soup, puree an additional cup or two of the bean mixture.

PREP: 10 MINUTES **UNDER PRESSURE:** 35 MINUTES **TOTAL:** 60 MINUTES

2 tablespoons olive oil, divided
1½ cups chopped red onion
1 tablespoon chili powder
1½ teaspoons ground cumin
2 garlic cloves, minced
1 pound dried black beans
3 cups water
½ teaspoon salt, divided
1 (32-ounce) carton fat-free, lower-sodium chicken broth
½ cup coarsely chopped fresh cilantro
¼ cup finely chopped red onion
2 tablespoons fresh lime juice
3 jalapeño peppers, seeded and minced
Light sour cream (optional)

1 Heat a 6-quart pressure cooker over medium-high heat. Add 1 tablespoon oil to cooker; swirl to coat. Add 1½ cups onion, chili powder, cumin, and garlic; sauté 2 minutes. Sort and wash beans. Add beans, 3 cups water, ⅜ teaspoon salt, and broth to cooker.

2 Close lid securely; bring to high pressure over high heat (about 8 minutes). Adjust heat to medium or level to maintain high pressure; cook 35 minutes. Remove from heat; let stand 8 minutes or until pressure releases. Remove lid.

3 While bean mixture stands, combine 1 tablespoon oil, ⅛ teaspoon salt, cilantro, and next 3 ingredients (through peppers) in a medium bowl; set aside.

4 Place 4 cups bean mixture in a blender. Remove center piece of blender lid (to allow steam to escape); secure blender lid on blender. Place a clean towel over opening in lid (to avoid splatters). Blend until smooth. Stir pureed bean mixture into remaining bean mixture in cooker.

5 Add about ½ cup cilantro mixture to bean mixture; stir gently. Divide soup among 8 bowls; top with cilantro relish and sour cream, if desired.

SERVES 8 (SERVING SIZE: ABOUT 1 CUP SOUP AND 2 TABLESPOONS RELISH)
CALORIES 250; **FAT** 4G (SAT 0.5G, MONO 2.7G, POLY 0.4G); **PROTEIN** 14G; **CARB** 42G; **FIBER** 15G; **CHOL** 0MG; **IRON** 5.3MG; **SODIUM** 440MG; **CALC** 98MG

Meatless
TIKKA MASALA

This delicious meatless recipe is a quick and easy swap
for the traditional chicken tikka masala.

PREP: 10 MINUTES **UNDER PRESSURE:** 32 MINUTES **TOTAL:** 1 HOUR 15 MINUTES

4 cups water, divided
¾ cup uncooked whole-wheat
   couscous
2 tablespoons canola oil,
   divided
1½ cups diced onion
1½ cups diced carrot
1½ teaspoons curry
   powder
1 teaspoon ground cumin
¼ teaspoon ground red
   pepper
8 ounces dried chickpeas
   (garbanzo beans)
1 cup frozen green peas
½ cup chopped fresh
   cilantro
1 tablespoon grated peeled
   fresh ginger
1 teaspoon sugar
¾ teaspoon salt
1 (14.5-ounce) can diced
   tomatoes, undrained
1 (13.5-ounce) can light
   coconut milk
1 lime, cut into 6 wedges

1 Bring 1¼ cups water to a boil in a 6-quart pressure cooker. Remove from heat, and stir in couscous. Cover (do not lock), and let stand 5 minutes. Fluff with a fork. Remove couscous from cooker; place in a medium bowl, and set aside.

2 Heat cooker over medium-high heat. Add 1 tablespoon oil to cooker; swirl to coat. Add onion; sauté 4 minutes or until browned. Add 1 tablespoon oil, carrot, and next 3 ingredients (through red pepper); cook 30 seconds, stirring constantly. Sort and wash chickpeas. Add chickpeas and 2¾ cups water to cooker.

3 Close lid securely; bring to high pressure over high heat (about 7 minutes). Adjust heat to medium or level to maintain high pressure; cook 32 minutes. Remove from heat; let stand 10 minutes or until pressure releases. Remove lid. Stir in green peas and next 6 ingredients (through coconut milk). Cook over medium-high heat 5 minutes or until thoroughly heated. Divide couscous among 6 shallow bowls; top with chickpea mixture, and serve with lime wedges.

SERVES 6 (SERVING SIZE: ⅓ CUP COUSCOUS, 1⅓ CUPS CHICKPEA MIXTURE, AND 1 LIME WEDGE)
CALORIES 370; **FAT** 12G (SAT 3.7G, MONO 3G, POLY 1.4G); **PROTEIN** 14G; **CARB** 56G; **FIBER** 14G; **CHOL** 0MG; **IRON** 4.2MG; **SODIUM** 500MG; **CALC** 89MG

Lemon, Wheat Berry, and
CHICKPEA SALAD

Look for wheat berries in the grain or bulk section of your supermarket.

PREP: 10 MINUTES **UNDER PRESSURE:** 27 MINUTES **TOTAL:** 1 HOUR 10 MINUTES

8 ounces dried chickpeas
(garbanzo beans)
8 ounces uncooked wheat
berries (hard winter wheat)
8 cups water
¼ cup extra-virgin olive oil,
divided
1½ cups frozen green peas
1½ cups diced English
cucumber
1 cup sliced bottled roasted
red bell pepper

¾ cup diced red onion
2 teaspoons grated lemon
rind
¼ cup fresh lemon juice
2 teaspoons dried dill
¼ teaspoon freshly ground
black pepper
4 ounces crumbled feta
cheese (about 1 cup)
1¼ teaspoons salt

1 Sort and wash chickpeas. Combine chickpeas, wheat berries, 8 cups water, and 1 tablespoon oil in a 6-quart pressure cooker. Close lid securely; bring to high pressure over high heat (about 20 minutes). Reduce heat to medium or level needed to maintain high pressure; cook 27 minutes. Remove from heat; let stand 13 minutes or until pressure releases. Remove lid.

2 While cooker stands, combine 3 tablespoons oil, peas, and next 7 ingredients (through black pepper) in a large bowl. Drain chickpea mixture through a fine sieve. Rinse with cold water; drain well. Add chickpea mixture to bowl; toss well. Stir in feta cheese and salt. Serve immediately, or cover and chill.

SERVES 10 (SERVING SIZE: 1 CUP)
CALORIES 270; **FAT** 9G (SAT 2G, MONO 4.3G, POLY 0.5G); **PROTEIN** 11G; **CARB** 36G; **FIBER** 8G; **CHOL** 5MG; **IRON** 3MG; **SODIUM** 450MG; **CALC** 82MG

5 MINUTE PREP!

COUNTRYSIDE
Black-Eyed Peas

Serve with warm corn bread for soaking up the peas' flavorful sauce.

PREP: 5 MINUTES   **UNDER PRESSURE:** 10 MINUTES   **TOTAL:** 45 MINUTES

2 tablespoons all-purpose flour
8 bacon slices, chopped
1½ cups diced onion
1 pound dried black-eyed peas
6 cups water
2 bay leaves
1 teaspoon salt
1 teaspoon thyme leaves
Hot sauce (optional)

1 Heat a 6-quart pressure cooker over medium heat. Add flour to cooker; cook 4 minutes or until light golden brown, stirring constantly with a whisk. (If flour browns too fast, remove cooker from heat; stir constantly until flour cools.) Remove flour from cooker; set aside.

2 Add bacon to cooker; cook over medium heat 8 minutes or until crisp. Remove bacon from cooker, reserving 2 tablespoons drippings in cooker. Drain bacon; pat dry with paper towels. Increase heat to medium-high. Add onion to drippings in cooker; sauté 3 minutes or until lightly browned. Sort and wash peas. Add peas, 6 cups water, and bay leaves to cooker.

3 Close lid securely; bring to high pressure over high heat (about 9 minutes). Adjust heat to medium or level to maintain high pressure; cook 10 minutes. Remove from heat; let stand 10 minutes or until pressure releases. Remove lid. Sprinkle pea mixture with flour and salt; stir with a whisk. Stir in bacon and thyme. Remove and discard bay leaves. Serve with hot sauce, if desired.

SERVES 7 (SERVING SIZE: 1 CUP)
CALORIES 290; **FAT** 7G (SAT 2.5G, MONO 1.7G, POLY 1.1G); **PROTEIN** 14G;
CARB 43G; **FIBER** 16G; **CHOL** 5MG; **IRON** 4MG; **SODIUM** 420MG; **CALC** 110MG

Spanish
CHICKPEA SOUP

Dried chickpeas are typically soaked overnight, and then simmered for up to 2½ hours to become tender. These, though, go into the pressure cooker dry and come out tender in just a little over an hour!

PREP: 5 MINUTES **UNDER PRESSURE:** 1 HOUR AND 15 MINUTES **TOTAL:** 1 HOUR AND 29 MINUTES

1 tablespoon olive oil
1½ cups chopped onion
4 ounces Spanish chorizo, diced
5 garlic cloves, minced
½ pound dried chickpeas (garbanzo beans)
3½ cups water
2½ cups fat-free, lower-sodium chicken broth
2 bay leaves
4 cups baby spinach
1 tablespoon sherry vinegar
½ teaspoon freshly ground black pepper
⅜ teaspoon kosher salt
¼ teaspoon crushed red pepper

1 Heat a 6-quart pressure cooker over medium-high heat. Add oil to cooker; swirl to coat. Add onion; sauté 3 minutes. Add chorizo and garlic; sauté 2 minutes. Sort and wash chickpeas. Add chickpeas and next 3 ingredients (through bay leaves) to cooker. Close lid securely; bring to high pressure over high heat (about 4 minutes). Adjust heat to medium or level needed to maintain high pressure; cook 1 hour and 15 minutes. Remove from heat; place cooker under cold running water. Remove lid. Remove bay leaves; discard. Add spinach and remaining ingredients, stirring just until spinach wilts. Serve immediately.

SERVES 6 (SERVING SIZE: 1⅓ CUPS)
CALORIES 250; **FAT** 8G (SAT 1.5G, MONO 1.8G, POLY 0.4G); **PROTEIN** 14G; **CARB** 34G; **FIBER** 9G; **CHOL** 10MG; **IRON** 4MG; **SODIUM** 500MG; **CALC** 72MG

PRESSURE PERFECT TIP:
Brown the onion, garlic, and sausage before cooking the chickpeas. The brown bits formed on the bottom of the pot give this dish its rich flavor.

QUICKER BEANS!

Here's how to cook your favorite dried beans in around 30 minutes. While cooking dried beans on the stovetop can take up to 2 hours of careful simmering to develop their tender texture, the pressure cooker can do the trick 3 times as fast.

START HERE!

1. Sort, wash, and soak ½ pound beans overnight. Combine soaked beans with 2 quarts water, ½ tablespoon oil, and ½ teaspoon salt in a 6-quart pressure cooker. Add your favorite seasonings.

2. Close lid securely; bring to desired pressure over medium-high heat and maintain pressure according to chart.

3. Remove from heat and let stand until pressure has released. If needed, simmer beans on stovetop until beans have reached desired tenderness.

BLACK BEANS
TOTAL TIME: 31 MINUTES
Cook under high pressure 9 minutes or low pressure 10 minutes.

CANNELLINI BEANS
TOTAL TIME: 27 MINUTES
Cook under high or low pressure 5 minutes.

BLACKEYED PEAS
TOTAL TIME: 27 MINUTES

Cook under high or low pressure 5 minutes.

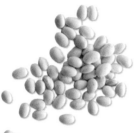

NAVY BEANS
TOTAL TIME: 30 MINUTES

Cook under high pressure 8 minutes or low pressure 10 minutes.

GARBANZO BEANS
TOTAL TIME: 25 MINUTES

Cook under high or low pressure 3 minutes.

GREAT NORTHERN BEANS
TOTAL TIME: 27 MINUTES

Cook under high or low pressure 5 minutes.

RED KIDNEY BEANS
TOTAL TIME: 27 MINUTES

Cook under high or low pressure 5 minutes.

Creamy Cannellini Beans with
GARLIC AND OREGANO

These beans are creamy, flavorful, and full of
protein. Don't worry if you don't have the herbs:
The garlic alone adds so much flavor.

PREP: 5 MINUTES **UNDER PRESSURE:** 5 MINUTES **TOTAL:** 30 MINUTES

1 pound dried cannellini
   beans
8 cups water
1¼ teaspoons kosher salt
¼ cup olive oil

¼ teaspoon dried oregano
2 garlic cloves, crushed
1 bay leaf
Freshly ground black pepper
   (optional)

1 Sort and wash beans; place in a 6-quart pressure cooker.
Add 8 cups water and salt. Close lid securely; bring to high
pressure over high heat (about 12 minutes). Adjust heat to
medium or level to maintain high pressure; cook 5 minutes.
Remove from heat; place cooker under cold running water.
Remove lid. Drain beans; discard cooking liquid.

2 Heat pan over medium heat. Add oil; swirl to coat. Add
oregano, garlic, and bay leaf; sauté 2 minutes or until garlic is
golden. Stir in bean mixture. Bring to a simmer; cook 4 minutes
or until creamy, stirring frequently. Remove from heat; remove
and discard garlic and bay leaf. Sprinkle with pepper, if desired.

SERVES 8 (SERVING SIZE: ½ CUP)
CALORIES 231; **FAT** 6.8G (SAT 0.9G, MONO 4.9G, POLY 0.7G); **PROTEIN** 12G;
CARB 30G; **FIBER** 8G; **CHOL** 0MG; **IRON** 6MG; **SODIUM** 310MG; **CALC** 102MG

WHITE BEAN,
Turkey Sausage, and Tortellini Soup
Add a small amount of chicken broth or water when reheating.

PREP: 5 MINUTES UNDER PRESSURE: 25 MINUTES TOTAL: 56 MINUTES

1 tablespoon canola oil
1 pound mild turkey Italian sausage, casings removed
4½ cups water
3½ cups fat-free, lower-sodium chicken broth
1 pound dried navy beans
1 cup chopped fennel bulb
1 teaspoon chopped fresh oregano
1½ cups diced red bell pepper
1 (9-ounce) package fresh three-cheese tortellini
3 cups arugula
¼ cup refrigerated reduced-fat pesto

1 Heat a 6-quart pressure cooker over medium-high heat. Add oil; swirl to coat. Add sausage, and cook 6 minutes or until browned, stirring to crumble. Drain sausage, and set aside.

2 Add 4½ cups water and broth to cooker, scraping pan to loosen browned bits. Sort and wash beans. Add beans, fennel, and oregano to cooker. Close lid securely; bring to high pressure over high heat (about 11 minutes). Adjust heat to medium or level to maintain high pressure; cook 25 minutes. Remove from heat; place cooker under cold running water. Remove lid. Bring bean mixture to a boil over high heat. Stir in cooked sausage, bell pepper, and tortellini; return to a boil over high heat. Reduce heat to low, and cook, uncovered, 7 minutes or until tortellini is done. Divide soup among bowls; top with arugula and pesto.

SERVES 12 (SERVING SIZE: 1 CUP SOUP, AND 1 TEASPOON PESTO)
CALORIES 290; FAT 9G (SAT 2.5G, MONO 0.9G, POLY 0.7G); PROTEIN 18G;
CARB 36G; FIBER 11G; CHOL 30MG; IRON 3MG; SODIUM 520MG; CALC 124MG

Red Pepper Soup
WITH GOUDA

Spicy, smoky, and velvety is the best way
to describe this simple soup. If you like a lot of heat,
use 2 teaspoons adobo sauce instead of just 1.

PREP: 10 MINUTES   UNDER PRESSURE: 5 MINUTES   TOTAL: 53 MINUTES

4 red bell peppers (about 1½ pounds), halved
1 tablespoon canola oil
1 cup diced onion
½ cup sliced carrot
½ cup sliced celery
½ teaspoon garlic powder
1 (14.5-ounce) can organic vegetable broth
1 (15.5-ounce) can unsalted navy beans, rinsed and drained
1 chipotle chile, canned in adobo sauce
1 teaspoon adobo sauce
1 cup half-and-half
1 ounce Gouda cheese, shredded (about ¼ cup)

1 Thinly slice 3 bell pepper halves and chop 2 bell pepper halves; set aside remaining bell pepper halves and chopped bell pepper. Heat a 6-quart pressure cooker over medium-high heat. Add oil; swirl to coat. Add sliced bell pepper to cooker; sauté 5 minutes or until browned.

2 Stir in remaining 3 bell pepper halves, onion, and next 7 ingredients (through adobo sauce). Close lid securely; bring to high pressure over high heat (about 8 minutes). Reduce heat to medium or level needed to maintain high pressure; cook 5 minutes. Remove from heat; let stand 18 minutes or until pressure releases. Remove lid; cool 15 minutes.

3 Place half of pepper mixture in a blender. Remove center piece of blender lid (to allow steam to escape); secure blender lid on blender. Place a clean towel over opening in blender lid (to avoid splatters). Blend until smooth. Pour into a large bowl. Repeat procedure with remaining pepper mixture. Return pureed mixture to cooker. Stir in half-and-half; cook over medium-high heat 2 to 3 minutes or until thoroughly heated. Ladle soup into bowls; sprinkle with cheese and remaining chopped bell pepper.

SERVES 6 (SERVING SIZE: 1 CUP SOUP AND ABOUT 2 TEASPOONS CHEESE)
CALORIES 231; FAT 6.8G (SAT 0.9G, MONO 4.9G, POLY 0.7G); PROTEIN 12G; CARB 30G; FIBER 8G; CHOL 0MG; IRON 6MG; SODIUM 310MG; CALC 102MG

SWAP IN A SNAP:
You can use other varieties of white beans like cannellini or Great Northern.

6 STEPS
to Perfectly Cooked
BEANS

The cooking times will vary depending upon what type of bean you use. But be sure to follow these foolproof tips for great beans every time you make them.

1. WASH AND SORT THE BEANS

Always wash the beans in a colander under running cold water to remove dirt. Gently run your hands through the beans to check for any unwanted debris or shriveled beans before cooking.

2. SOAK THE BEANS OVERNIGHT

Most recipes in this chapter don't require this step, but soaking the beans in water overnight softens them, which reduces the cooking time by a third.

3. ADD SALT

Adding salt to the soaking and cooking liquid tenderizes the beans, helping them to cook faster. For sodium control, you can omit the salt—just plan to cook them under pressure a few extra minutes.

4. USE OIL

Adding oil to the liquid helps prevent the cooking liquid from foaming and the beans from clumping together. It also adds flavor and gives body to the cooking liquid.

5. USE AMPLE LIQUID

Having enough liquid (water or broth) in the pot ensures even cooking. The amount used also impacts the time it takes for the pot to come to pressure and the total cooking time.

6. REMOVE FLOATING BEANS

Undercooked beans can often float to the top of the water after you release the pressure. It's best to just remove them by skimming the liquid with a slotted spoon or sieve.

Tomato-Kalamata
WHITE BEAN PASTA

A dense pasta, like a shell-shaped variety,
holds up well when cooked under pressure and achieves
an adequate texture in just 2 minutes.

PREP: 5 MINUTES   **UNDER PRESSURE:** 23 MINUTES   **TOTAL:** 40 MINUTES

2 cups grape tomatoes, halved
1 cup chopped fresh basil
½ cup chopped pitted kalamata olives (about 34 olives)
2 tablespoons extra-virgin olive oil
8 ounces dried navy beans
7 cups water
2 cups chopped onion
1 tablespoon extra-virgin olive oil
3 teaspoons chopped fresh rosemary
2 garlic cloves, chopped
1 (12-ounce) package white fiber mini shell pasta
½ teaspoon salt
4 ounces crumbled feta cheese (about 1 cup)

1 Combine first 4 ingredients in a medium bowl; set aside.

2 Sort and wash beans. Combine beans, 7 cups water, and next 4 ingredients (through garlic) in a 6-quart pressure cooker. Close lid securely; bring to high pressure over high heat (about 7 minutes). Adjust heat to medium or level needed to maintain high pressure; cook 20 minutes. Remove from heat; place cooker under cold running water. Remove lid.

3 Add pasta to bean mixture in cooker. Close lid securely; bring to high pressure over high heat (about 2 minutes). Adjust heat to medium or level needed to maintain high pressure; cook 3 minutes. Remove from heat; place cooker under cold running water. Remove lid. Add salt to pasta mixture; toss gently.

4 Divide pasta mixture among 8 shallow bowls; top with tomato mixture and cheese.

SERVES 8 (SERVING SIZE: ABOUT 1 CUP PASTA MIXTURE, ABOUT ⅓ CUP TOMATO MIXTURE, AND ABOUT 2 TABLESPOONS CHEESE)
CALORIES 350; **FAT** 13G (SAT 3G, MONO 7.4G, POLY 1.3G); **PROTEIN** 14G; **CARB** 56G; **FIBER** 13G; **CHOL** 10MG; **IRON** 3MG; **SODIUM** 710MG; **CALC** 273MG

WHITE BEANS
with Roasted Red Pepper and Pesto

PREP: 10 MINUTES **UNDER PRESSURE:** 15 MINUTES **TOTAL:** 45 MINUTES

2 cups loosely packed basil leaves

2 ounces grated fresh Parmesan cheese (about ½ cup)

2 tablespoons pine nuts, toasted

2 tablespoons water

2 tablespoons extra-virgin olive oil

¼ teaspoon salt

⅛ teaspoon freshly ground black pepper

1 garlic clove, crushed

1 pound dried Great Northern beans

10 cups water, divided

1½ cups coarsely chopped onion

1 tablespoon chopped fresh sage

1 tablespoon extra-virgin olive oil

2 garlic cloves, crushed

1 tablespoon balsamic vinegar

1 teaspoon salt

¼ teaspoon freshly ground black pepper

1 (12-ounce) bottle roasted red bell peppers, drained and chopped

1 To make pesto, place first 8 ingredients (through garlic) in a blender or food processor; process until smooth.

2 Sort and wash beans. Combine beans and 4 cups water in a 6-quart pressure cooker. Close lid securely; bring to high pressure over high heat (about 7 minutes). Adjust heat to medium or level needed to maintain high pressure; cook 3 minutes. Remove from heat; place cooker under cold running water. Remove lid. Drain beans; discard cooking liquid.

3 Combine beans, 6 cups water, onion, and next 3 ingredients (through garlic) in cooker. Close lid securely; bring to high pressure over high heat (about 7 minutes). Adjust heat to medium or level needed to maintain high pressure; cook 12 minutes. Remove from heat; place cooker under cold running water. Remove lid; let bean mixture stand 10 minutes. Drain bean mixture in a colander over a bowl, reserving 1 cup cooking liquid. Return bean mixture and 1 cup cooking liquid to cooker. Stir in vinegar and next 3 ingredients (through bell pepper). Spoon bean mixture into bowls; top with pesto.

SERVES 7 (SERVING SIZE: 1 CUP BEAN MIXTURE AND 2 TABLESPOONS PESTO)
CALORIES 350; **FAT** 11G (SAT 2.5G, MONO 5.7G, POLY 1.8G); **PROTEIN** 18G; **CARB** 48G; **FIBER** 14G; **CHOL** 5MG; **IRON** 4.7MG; **SODIUM** 290MG; **CALC** 241MG

PRESSURE PERFECT TIP:
For the best flavor, use an aged balsamic vinegar.

15 MINUTE PREP!

RED BEANS AND RICE

PREP: 15 MINUTES   UNDER PRESSURE: 5 MINUTES   TOTAL: 40 MINUTES

1 pound dried red kidney beans
8 cups water
1 tablespoon olive oil
1 pound andouille sausage, cut into ¾-inch pieces
1½ cups chopped onion
1½ cups chopped poblano chile
1 cup diced celery
2 tablespoons chopped fresh thyme
½ teaspoon kosher salt
10 garlic cloves, crushed

1 (12-ounce) can beer
4 cups unsalted chicken stock
½ teaspoon ground red pepper
¼ teaspoon freshly ground black pepper
3 bay leaves
½ cup thinly sliced green onions, divided
2 tablespoons cider vinegar
4 cups hot cooked long-grain rice

1 Sort and wash beans; place in a 6-quart pressure cooker. Add 8 cups water. Close lid securely; bring to high pressure over high heat (about 12 minutes). Adjust heat to medium or level to maintain high pressure; cook 5 minutes. Remove from heat; place cooker under cold running water. Remove lid. Drain beans; discard cooking liquid.

2 Return pressure cooker (lid unattached) to medium-high heat. Add oil to pan; swirl to coat. Add sausage; cook 6 minutes or until browned. Add onion and next 5 ingredients (through garlic); cook 8 minutes. Stir in beer; bring to a boil. Cook 2 minutes, scraping pan to loosen browned bits. Add beans, stock, red pepper, black pepper, and bay leaves. Simmer 10 minutes. Remove and discard bay leaves. Stir in ¼ cup green onions and vinegar. Serve over rice; sprinkle with ¼ cup green onions.

SERVES 8 (SERVING SIZE: 1 CUP BEAN MIXTURE, AND ½ CUP RICE)
CALORIES 380; **FAT** 4.5G (SAT 0.5G, MONO 1.8G, POLY 0.5G); **PROTEIN** 21G; **CARB** 66G; **FIBER** 15G; **CHOL** 20MG; **IRON** 4.2MG; **SODIUM** 670MG; **CALC** 94MG

BOURBON BAKED BEANS

PREP: 10 MINUTES   UNDER PRESSURE: 8 MINUTES   TOTAL: 50 MINUTES

10 MINUTE PREP!

1 pound dried navy beans
3 applewood-smoked bacon
   slices
1 cup finely chopped onion
7 cups water, divided
1/2 cup maple syrup, divided
1/4 cup plus 2 tablespoons
   bourbon, divided
1/4 cup Dijon mustard
1 1/2 teaspoons
   Worcestershire sauce
1/4 teaspoon freshly ground
   black pepper
1 tablespoon cider vinegar
1 teaspoon salt
1/4 cup chopped green onion

1 Sort and wash beans; place in a large Dutch oven.

2 Heat a 6-quart pressure cooker over medium-high heat. Add bacon to pan, and cook 4 minutes or until crisp. Remove from pan, reserving 1½ tablespoons drippings in pan; crumble bacon. Add onion to drippings in pan; cook 5 minutes or until onion begins to brown, stirring frequently. Add beans, bacon, 6 cups water, ¼ cup maple syrup, ¼ cup bourbon, and next 3 ingredients (through pepper) to pan.

3 Close lid securely; bring to high pressure over high heat (about 7 minutes). Adjust heat to medium or level to maintain high pressure; cook 8 minutes. Remove from heat; place cooker under cold running water. Remove lid. Drain beans; discard cooking liquid.

4 Return beans to pan. Stir in 1 cup water, ¼ cup maple syrup, and 2 tablespoons bourbon. Simmer 15 minutes until beans are tender and liquid is almost absorbed. Stir in vinegar and salt. Sprinkle with green onions before serving.

SERVES 13 (SERVING SIZE: ½ CUP)
CALORIES 190; **FAT** 1.5G (SAT 0G, MONO 0.6G, POLY 0.5G); **PROTEIN** 9G;
CARB 32G; **FIBER** 9G; **CHOL** 5MG; **IRON** 2MG; **SODIUM** 360MG; **CALC** 68MG

REFRIED BEANS

Enjoy these beans as a side dish
along with your favorite Mexican entrée, an appetizer
accompanied by chips, or a filling for burritos.

PREP: 5 MINUTES   **UNDER PRESSURE:** 48 MINUTES   **TOTAL:** 1 HOUR 20 MINUTES

1 pound dried pinto beans
20 cups water, divided
2 ounces diced ham
2 garlic cloves, minced
2 tablespoons canola oil
1¼ teaspoons salt
6 ounces sharp cheddar
   cheese, shredded
   (about 1½ cups)
Cilantro sprigs (optional)

1 Sort and wash beans; place in a 6-quart pressure cooker. Add 10 cups water. Close lid securely; bring to high pressure over high heat (about 12 minutes). Adjust heat to medium or level to maintain high pressure; cook 3 minutes. Remove from heat; place cooker under cold running water. Remove lid. Drain beans; discard cooking liquid.

2 Return beans to cooker. Add 10 cups water, ham, and garlic. Close lid securely; bring to high pressure over high heat (about 7 minutes). Adjust heat to medium or level to maintain high pressure; cook 45 minutes. Remove from heat; place cooker under cold running water. Remove lid. Drain beans, reserving 1 cup cooking liquid.

3 Heat a large skillet over medium heat. Add oil, beans, 1 cup cooking liquid, and salt. Mash bean mixture to desired consistency with a potato masher. Cook 5 minutes or until thoroughly heated, stirring occasionally. Sprinkle with cheese and if desired, cilantro.

SERVES 10 (SERVING SIZE: ABOUT ½ CUP BEANS AND ABOUT 2 TABLESPOONS CHEESE)
CALORIES 290; **FAT** 9G (SAT 4.5G, MONO 1.8G, POLY 0.8G); **PROTEIN** 15G;
CARB 33G; **FIBER** 12G; **CHOL** 20MG; **IRON** 3MG; **SODIUM** 373MG; **CALC** 195MG

SWAP IN A SNAP:
Chop two uncooked
slices of bacon, and use
instead of the ham.

HEARTY GRAINS

Ground Corn
BREAKFAST BOWLS

Try this "no-stir" method for making creamy grits.
Serve with eggs and bacon for a heartier meal.

PREP: 10 MINUTES   **UNDER PRESSURE:** 22 MINUTES   **TOTAL:** 40 MINUTES

1 cup stone-ground cornmeal
3¾ cups water, divided
1 cup 2% reduced-fat milk
1 tablespoon canola oil
1 garlic clove, chopped
½ teaspoon salt
½ teaspoon Worcestershire sauce
⅛ teaspoon ground red pepper
4 ounces reduced-fat sharp cheddar cheese, shredded (about 1 cup)
¼ cup chopped green onions

1 Combine cornmeal, 2 cups water, milk, oil, and garlic in a 4-cup glass measure. Pour 1¾ cups water into a 6-quart pressure cooker. Place a trivet or cooking rack in cooker. Place 4-cup glass measure on top of trivet.

2 Close lid securely; bring to high pressure over high heat (about 6 minutes). Adjust heat to medium or level to maintain high pressure; cook 22 minutes. Remove from heat; let stand 6 minutes or until pressure releases. Remove lid.

3 Stir in salt, Worcestershire sauce, and pepper. Gradually add ¾ cup cheese, stirring until cheese melts. Garnish with chopped green onions and remaining shredded cheese.

SERVES 4 (SERVING SIZE: 1 CUP)
CALORIES 260; **FAT** 10G (SAT 4G, MONO 2.6G, POLY 1.0.G); **PROTEIN** 10G;
CARB 31G; **FIBER** 2G; **CHOL** 20MG; **IRON** 2MG; **SODIUM** 570MG; **CALC** 227MG

PRESSURE PERFECT TIP:
For a thinner consistency, stir in 2 to 3 tablespoons additional milk at the end.

Peanutty
MAPLE OATS

Peanut butter and maple syrup elevate the flavor and satisfaction of this morning staple.

PREP: 10 MINUTES   **UNDER PRESSURE:** 2 MINUTES   **TOTAL:** 22 MINUTES

1 cup steel-cut oats
3 cups water
1 tablespoon canola oil
⅛ teaspoon salt
½ cup plus 1 tablespoon reduced-fat peanut butter
1½ cups diced banana
¼ cup pure maple syrup
⅛ teaspoon ground nutmeg

1 Combine first 4 ingredients (through salt) in a 6-quart pressure cooker. Close lid securely; bring to high pressure over high heat (about 5 minutes). Adjust heat to medium or level needed to maintain high pressure; cook 2 minutes. Remove from heat; let stand 9 minutes or until pressure releases. Remove lid; stir in peanut butter.

2 Divide oats mixture among 6 bowls. Top with banana, and drizzle with syrup. Sprinkle with nutmeg, and serve immediately.

SERVES 6 (SERVING SIZE: ABOUT ½ CUP OATS MIXTURE, ¼ CUP BANANA, AND 2 TEASPOONS MAPLE SYRUP)
CALORIES 320; **FAT** 13G (SAT 2.5G, MONO 1.5G, POLY 0.7G); **PROTEIN** 10G; **CARB** 47G; **FIBER** 5G; **CHOL** 0MG; **IRON** 2MG; **SODIUM** 240MG; **CALC** 28MG

SWAP IN A SNAP:
Try dried blueberries, cranberries, or raisins in place of the banana—they offer a nice chewy texture.

BROWN RICE CEREAL
with Vanilla Cream and Berries

Serve hot, at room temperature, or cold. To make ahead for a breakfast on the go, store in the refrigerator for up to 3 days.

PREP: 10 MINUTES   **UNDER PRESSURE:** 9 MINUTES   **TOTAL:** 25 MINUTES

1 cup uncooked long-grain brown rice
5 cups water
1 tablespoon canola oil
⅛ teaspoon salt
1 cup fat-free milk
¼ cup heavy cream

3 tablespoons sugar
1 teaspoon vanilla extract
½ cup fresh blueberries
½ cup fresh raspberries
2 teaspoons grated lemon rind

1 Heat a 6-quart pressure cooker over medium-high heat. Add rice; cook 2 minutes or until toasted, stirring frequently. Add 5 cups water and oil.

2 Close lid securely; bring to high pressure over high heat (about 6 minutes). Adjust heat to medium or level to maintain high pressure; cook 9 minutes. Remove from heat; place cooker under cold running water. Remove lid. Drain rice through a sieve. Add salt to rice in sieve.

3 Combine milk, cream, and sugar in cooker; cook over medium heat 1½ minutes or until thoroughly heated. Remove from heat; stir in vanilla.

4 Divide rice among 4 bowls; top with milk mixture. Sprinkle with berries and lemon rind.

SERVES 4 (SERVING SIZE: ABOUT ⅔ CUP RICE, ABOUT ⅓ CUP MILK MIXTURE, ¼ CUP BERRIES, AND ½ TEASPOON LEMON RIND)
CALORIES 320; **FAT** 9G (SAT 4G, MONO 3.2G, POLY 1.3G); **PROTEIN** 7G; **CARB** 54G; **FIBER** 4G; **CHOL** 20MG; **IRON** 0.1MG; **SODIUM** 120MG; **CALC** 154MG

TOASTED ALMOND and APPLE QUINOA

Jump-start your morning with a bowl of warm quinoa cereal. It's loaded with protein and fiber, which will keep you satisfied throughout the morning.

PREP: 5 MINUTES **UNDER PRESSURE:** 5 MINUTES **TOTAL:** 17 MINUTES

²/₃ cup slivered almonds
1 cup uncooked quinoa
2 cups water
¹/₃ cup dried tart cherries
1 tablespoon canola oil
¹/₄ teaspoon salt
1 teaspoon vanilla extract
1 cup sliced Braeburn apple
1 tablespoon sugar
¹/₄ teaspoon ground cinnamon

1 Heat a 6-quart pressure cooker over medium-high heat. Add almonds; cook 2 to 3 minutes or until lightly browned, stirring frequently. Remove from cooker, and set aside.

2 Add quinoa to cooker; cook over medium-high heat 1 minute or until lightly browned, stirring frequently. Stir in 2 cups water and next 3 ingredients (through salt).

3 Close lid securely; bring to high pressure over high heat (about 1 minute). Adjust heat to medium or level to maintain high pressure; cook 5 minutes. Remove from heat; let stand 3 to 4 minutes or until pressure releases. Remove lid; stir in vanilla.

4 While cooker stands, combine almonds, apple, sugar, and cinnamon, tossing to coat. Divide quinoa mixture among 4 bowls; top with apple mixture.

SERVES 4 (SERVING SIZE: ²/₃ CUP QUINOA MIXTURE AND ABOUT ¹/₃ CUP APPLE MIXTURE)
CALORIES 310; **FAT** 9G (SAT 0G, MONO 3.8G, POLY 1.5G); **PROTEIN** 9G; **CARB** 46G; **FIBER** 13G; **CHOL** 0MG; **IRON** 3MG; **SODIUM** 160MG; **CALC** 30MG

Rustic Vegetable-Barley Soup
WITH CROUTONS

PREP: 28 MINUTES   UNDER PRESSURE: 9 MINUTES   TOTAL: 37 MINUTES

3 ounces multigrain Italian bread, cut into ½-inch cubes

2 tablespoons olive oil, divided

1⅓ cups chopped onion

1 cup half-moon–sliced carrot

1 cup finely chopped red bell pepper

1½ cups water

⅔ cup uncooked pearl barley, rinsed and drained

1 tablespoon chopped fresh basil

2 tablespoons tomato paste

½ teaspoon freshly ground black pepper

8 ounces mushrooms, quartered

5 ounces fresh green beans, trimmed and cut into 1-inch pieces

1 (14.5-ounce) can organic vegetable broth

1 (14.5-ounce) can unsalted diced tomatoes with basil, garlic, and oregano, undrained

3 ounces part-skim mozzarella cheese, shredded (about ¾ cup)

1½ ounces fresh Parmesan cheese, shredded (about 6 tablespoons)

1 Preheat oven to 400°.

2 Place bread cubes in a large bowl; drizzle with 1 tablespoon oil, tossing gently to coat. Arrange bread cubes in a single layer on a jelly-roll pan. Bake at 400° for 8 to 10 minutes or until toasted, stirring gently after 4 minutes.

3 Heat a 6-quart pressure cooker over medium-high heat. Add 1 tablespoon oil to cooker; swirl to coat. Add onion, carrot, and bell pepper; sauté 3 minutes or until tender. Stir in 1½ cups water and next 8 ingredients (through tomatoes).

4 Close lid securely; bring to high pressure over high heat (about 9 minutes). Adjust heat to medium or level to maintain high pressure; cook 9 minutes. Remove from heat; place cooker under cold running water. Remove lid.

5 Divide barley mixture among 6 bowls; top with mozzarella cheese, Parmesan cheese, and croutons.

SERVES 6 (SERVING SIZE: ABOUT 1⅓ CUPS SOUP, 2 TABLESPOONS MOZZARELLA CHEESE, 1 TABLESPOON PARMESAN CHEESE, AND ABOUT ⅓ CUP CROUTONS)

CALORIES 271; **FAT** 5.9G (SAT 1.2G, MONO 2.2G, POLY 1.6G); **PROTEIN** 10G; **CARB** 32G; **FIBER** 7G; **CHOL** 0MG; **IRON** 6MG; **SODIUM** 310MG; **CALC** 102MG

QUICKER GRAINS!

Here's how to cook your favorite long-cooking grains in less than 30 minutes. The pressure cooker cuts the cooking time for a wide variety of grains by at least half as compared to the traditional stovetop method.

START HERE!

1. Toss desired grain with 1 tablespoon oil, and sprinkle with ¾ teaspoon salt. Combine 1 cup grain mixture and 3 quarts water in a 6-quart pressure cooker.

2. Close lid securely; bring to desired pressure over medium-high heat (about 4 minutes) and maintain pressure according to chart.

3. Remove from heat; release pressure according to chart. If needed, simmer cooked grains on stovetop until desired tenderness is reached. Drain and add your favorite seasonings.

QUINOA
TOTAL TIME: 6 MINUTES
Cook under high or low pressure 1 minute.

LONG-GRAIN BROWN RICE
TOTAL TIME: 12 MINUTES
Cook under high pressure 7 minutes.

WILD RICE

TOTAL TIME: 23 MINUTES

Cook under high pressure 18 minutes or low pressure 22 minutes.

FARRO

TOTAL TIME: 11 MINUTES

Cook under high pressure 6 minutes or low pressure 7 minutes.

PEARL BARLEY

TOTAL TIME: 14 MINUTES

Cook under high pressure 9 minutes.

RED QUINOA

TOTAL TIME: 10 MINUTES

Cook under high or low pressure 5 minutes.

WHEAT BERRIES

TOTAL TIME: 15 MINUTES

Cook under high pressure 10 minutes or low pressure 12 minutes.

BARLEY, SALAMI, and ARTICHOKE SALAD

This dish makes a great "weeklong" entrée salad, perfect for brown bagging. Add a small amount of vinegar to lift the flavors after a day or two.

PREP: 10 MINUTES   **UNDER PRESSURE:** 9 MINUTES   **TOTAL:** 31 MINUTES

6 cups water

8 ounces uncooked pearl barley, rinsed and drained

⅓ cup extra-virgin olive oil, divided

2 cups grape tomatoes, halved lengthwise

2 cups finely chopped kale

1 cup diced red onion

4 ounces hard salami slices (such as Oscar Meyer), cut into very thin strips

2 ounces pepperoncini peppers, drained and thinly sliced (about ½ cup)

¼ cup cider vinegar

2 tablespoons chopped fresh oregano

1 (14-ounce) can quartered artichoke hearts, drained

6 ounces fresh Parmesan or Asiago cheese, shredded (about 1½ cups)

1 Combine 6 cups water, barley, and 1½ tablespoons oil in a 6-quart pressure cooker. Close lid securely; bring to high pressure over high heat (about 12 minutes). Adjust heat to medium or level to maintain high pressure; cook 9 minutes. Remove from heat; place cooker under cold running water. Remove lid.

2 While barley cooks, combine remaining oil, tomatoes, and next 7 ingredients (through artichoke hearts) in a large bowl. Drain barley through a fine sieve, and rinse with cold water; drain. Add barley to tomato mixture; toss gently. Serve immediately, or cover and chill until ready to serve. Sprinkle with cheese just before serving.

SERVES 10 (SERVING SIZE: 1 CUP BARLEY MIXTURE AND ABOUT 2½ TABLESPOONS CHEESE)
CALORIES 285; **FAT** 8.3G (SAT 0.7G, MONO 5.9G, POLY 0.7G); **PROTEIN** 14G; **CARB** 42G; **FIBER** 8G; **CHOL** 0MG; **IRON** 6MG; **SODIUM** 310MG; **CALC** 102MG

SWAP IN A SNAP:
Kalamata or green Spanish olives make a good substitute for the artichokes.

Cheddar-Fontina
PENNE

For a smooth sauce, be sure to combine the flour and water before adding it to the pot.

PREP: 21 MINUTES   UNDER PRESSURE: 3 MINUTES   TOTAL: 24 MINUTES

1 tablespoon plus 1 teaspoon extra-virgin olive oil, divided

1/2 cup panko (Japanese breadcrumbs)

3 3/4 cups water, divided

1 (14.5-ounce) package multi-grain penne (tube-shaped pasta)

2/3 cup evaporated low-fat milk

3/4 teaspoon garlic powder

3/4 teaspoon salt

1/4 teaspoon freshly ground black pepper

1/4 teaspoon ground red pepper

2 teaspoons all-purpose flour

3 ounces sharp white cheddar cheese, shredded (about 3/4 cup)

3 ounces fontina cheese, shredded (about 3/4 cup)

1 cup grape tomatoes, halved

1/4 cup finely chopped green onions

1 Heat a 6-quart pressure cooker over medium-high heat. Add 1 tablespoon oil to cooker; swirl to coat. Add panko; cook 1 minute or until golden brown, stirring constantly. Remove panko from cooker; set aside. Wipe cooker clean with a paper towel.

2 Combine 3½ cups water and pasta in cooker. Close lid securely; bring to high pressure over high heat (about 5 minutes). Adjust heat to medium or level to maintain high pressure; cook 3 minutes. Remove from heat, and place cooker under cold running water. Remove lid.

3 Remove pasta with a slotted spoon; place in a medium bowl. Add milk and next 4 ingredients (through red pepper) to cooking liquid. Combine ¼ cup water and flour in a small bowl; gradually add to milk mixture, stirring with a whisk. Bring to a simmer over medium-high heat; cook 2 minutes or until slightly thick. Remove from heat; add cheeses, stirring until cheeses melt. Stir in cooked pasta, tossing gently to coat.

4 Heat a medium nonstick skillet over medium-high heat. Add 1 teaspoon oil to pan; swirl to coat. Add tomatoes; sauté 2 minutes or until soft. Sprinkle pasta mixture with panko; top with tomatoes and green onions.

SERVES 6 (SERVING SIZE: 1½ CUPS)
CALORIES 330; FAT 5.8G (SAT 0.9G, MONO 3.9G, POLY 0.7G); PROTEIN 15G; CARB 45G; FIBER 8G; CHOL 0MG; IRON 6MG; SODIUM 310MG; CALC 102MG

10 MINUTE PREP!

Summer Pea, Watermelon, and FARRO SALAD

This unusual yet delicious combination of flavors makes a delightful substitute for traditional pasta salad at your next cookout.

PREP: 10 MINUTES   **UNDER PRESSURE:** 10 MINUTES   **TOTAL:** 31 MINUTES

3 cups water

1 cup uncooked farro or wheat berries

1 cup shelled green peas (about ¾ pound unshelled)

½ teaspoon salt

¼ teaspoon freshly ground black pepper

1 cup cubed seeded watermelon

1 cup coarsely chopped fresh flat-leaf parsley

1½ ounces fresh pecorino Romano cheese, shaved (about ⅓ cup)

1 Place 3 cups water and 1 cup uncooked farro in a pressure cooker. Close lid securely; bring to high pressure over high heat (about 10 minutes). Adjust heat to medium or level needed to maintain pressure; cook 11 minutes. Remove from heat; allow pressure to release naturally through steam vent. Remove lid; add green peas to pan with farro. Let stand 2 to 3 minutes or until crisp-tender.

2 Drain. Rinse farro mixture with cold water; drain.

3 Combine farro mixture, ½ teaspoon salt, and ¼ teaspoon black pepper in a large bowl. Add the watermelon cubes and 1 cup chopped parsley, and toss gently to combine. Top salad with Romano cheese.

SERVES 4 (SERVING SIZE: 1 CUP)
CALORIES 188; **FAT** 4.2G (SAT 1.9G, MONO 0.9G, POLY 0.2G); **PROTEIN** 10G; **CARB** 35G; **FIBER** 6G; **CHOL** 11MG; **IRON** 1.7MG; **SODIUM** 433MG; **CALC** 146MG

TOASTED MILLET
with Cilantro Vinaigrette

PREP: 7 MINUTES   UNDER PRESSURE: 24 MINUTES   TOTAL: 36 MINUTES

1½ teaspoons olive oil
½ cup chopped onion
1 cup uncooked millet
3 garlic cloves, minced
1 cup unsalted chicken stock
1 cup water
½ teaspoon kosher salt
2½ tablespoons olive oil
¼ teaspoon kosher salt
½ cup chopped fresh cilantro
2 tablespoons fresh lime juice
1 teaspoon honey
½ teaspoon cumin
¼ teaspoon black pepper
1 cup chopped red bell pepper
¾ cup diced avocado
1½ cups unsalted black beans
2 ounces crumbled feta cheese (about ½ cup)

1 Heat a 6-quart pressure cooker over medium-high heat. Add 1½ teaspoons oil to cooker; swirl to coat. Add onion; sauté 3 minutes. Add millet and garlic to pan; cook 2 minutes. Stir in chicken stock, 1 cup water, and ½ teaspoon kosher salt.

2 Close lid securely; bring to high pressure over medium-high heat (about 4 minutes). Adjust heat to low or level to maintain high pressure; cook 24 minutes. Remove from heat; place cooker under cold running water. Remove lid. Drain any remaining cooking liquid, if necessary.

3 Stir together 2½ tablespoons olive oil, ¼ teaspoon kosher salt, cilantro, lime juice, honey, cumin, and black pepper in a large bowl. Add millet. Add chopped red bell pepper, avocado, and black beans; toss to coat. Sprinkle with feta.

SERVES 8 (SERVING SIZE: ¾ CUP)
CALORIES 225; **FAT** 9.8G (SAT 2.3G, MONO 5.6G, POLY 1.4G); **PROTEIN** 7G;
CARB 28G; **FIBER** 5G; **CHOL** 0MG; **IRON** 0MG; **SODIUM** 283MG; **CALC** 0MG

WARM WILD RICE SALAD

Easy to make in advance, this grain-based salad can also be served cold. Simply cook the rice, chill, and toss with the remaining ingredients just before serving.

PREP: 9 MINUTES   UNDER PRESSURE: 24 MINUTES   TOTAL: 40 MINUTES

5 tablespoons olive oil, divided
½ cup chopped onion
3 garlic cloves, chopped and divided
1 cup uncooked wild rice
1 bay leaf
1½ cups fat-free, lower-sodium chicken broth
1½ cups water
½ cup chopped yellow bell pepper
⅓ cup sliced green onions
¼ cup sweetened dried cranberries, chopped
¼ cup pine nuts, toasted and chopped
2½ tablespoons cider vinegar
1 teaspoon honey
¼ teaspoon salt
¼ teaspoon freshly ground black pepper

1 Heat a 6-quart pressure cooker over medium-high heat. Add 1 tablespoon oil to cooker; swirl to coat. Add onion and 1 teaspoon garlic; sauté 3 minutes or until tender. Add rice and bay leaf, stirring to coat rice with oil. Stir in broth and 1½ cups water.

2 Close lid securely; bring to high pressure over medium-high heat (about 4 minutes). Adjust heat to low or level to maintain high pressure; cook 24 minutes. Remove from heat; place cooker under cold running water. Remove lid. Drain any remaining cooking liquid, if necessary. Remove bay leaf; discard. Stir in bell pepper and next 3 ingredients (through pine nuts).

3 Combine ¼ cup oil, 1 teaspoon garlic, vinegar, and next 3 ingredients (through black pepper) in a medium bowl, stirring with a whisk. Add rice mixture to dressing, tossing to coat. Serve warm.

SERVES 6 (SERVING SIZE: ⅔ CUP)
CALORIES 250; **FAT** 7.8G (SAT 0.9G, MONO 4.9G, POLY 0.7G); **PROTEIN** 12G; **CARB** 30G; **FIBER** 8G; **CHOL** 0MG; **IRON** 6MG; **SODIUM** 310MG; **CALC** 102MG

SWAP IN A SNAP:

Substitute farro for the wild rice. Just reduce the amount of time that this dish cooks under pressure to 15 minutes.

Edamame, Chicken, AND RICE SALAD

Cooking the chicken in a single layer allows the chicken to brown and not stew. The brown bits left behind help to season the rice.

PREP: 9 MINUTES   **UNDER PRESSURE:** 7 MINUTES   **TOTAL:** 43 MINUTES

2 tablespoons canola oil, divided
1 pound skinless, boneless chicken breast, cut into bite-sized pieces
1 cup uncooked long-grain brown rice
5 cups water
3 cups small broccoli florets
3/4 cup diced red onion
1 1/2 cups diced red bell pepper
1 cup chopped peanuts, toasted
1/2 cup frozen shelled edamame, thawed
1/3 cup lower-sodium soy sauce
1/3 cup rice vinegar
1/4 cup chopped fresh cilantro
1 1/2 tablespoons sugar
1 tablespoon grated peeled fresh ginger
1/2 teaspoon salt

1 Heat a 6-quart pressure cooker over medium-high heat. Add 1 tablespoon oil to cooker; swirl to coat. Add chicken to cooker in a single layer, and cook 2 minutes; stir and cook 4 minutes or until done. Remove chicken from cooker; set aside.

2 Add 1 tablespoon oil, rice, and 5 cups water to cooker, scraping cooker to loosen browned bits.

3 Close lid securely; bring to high pressure over high heat (about 7 minutes). Adjust heat to medium or level to maintain high pressure; cook 7 minutes. Remove from heat; place cooker under cold running water. Remove lid. Stir in broccoli; let stand 30 seconds. Drain rice mixture through a fine sieve; rinse with cold water, and drain well.

4 While rice mixture cooks, place onion in a medium bowl. Add cold water to cover; let stand 10 minutes. Drain.

5 Place rice mixture in a large bowl. Add chicken, onion, bell pepper, and remaining ingredients, tossing gently.

SERVES 8 (SERVING SIZE: ABOUT 1 CUP)
CALORIES 231; **FAT** 6.8G (SAT 0.9G, MONO 4.9G, POLY 0.7G); **PROTEIN** 12G; **CARB** 30G; **FIBER** 8G; **CHOL** 0MG; **IRON** 6MG; **SODIUM** 310MG; **CALC** 102MG

6 STEPS
to Perfectly Cooked
GRAINS

The right proportion of ingredients and cooking times will vary depending upon what variety of grain you use. But certain techniques will always yield the best results.

1. RINSE BEFORE COOKING

Rinsing grains before cooking helps to remove their powdery, starchy coating. This step keeps them from sticking together and also prevents the cooking water from foaming, which can cause the pressure valve to clog.

2. SOAK THE GRAIN

Soaking long-cooking grains before preparing them will speed up their cooking time. However, if you'd like to skip this step just plan to cook them a little longer.

3. ADD OIL

Using oil when cooking grains is key to preventing them from clumping, and it also reduces the amount of starchy foam that forms during cooking.

4. USE SALT

To enhance flavor, sprinkle the salt into the cooking liquid rather than adding it to the finished grains. This will ensure the salt absorbs into the grain, making for a more tasty dish.

5. BUILD FLAVOR

Before adding grains to the pot, build flavor by sautéing onion and/or garlic in the pot. You can also throw in a few spices and fresh ingredients like lemon zest.

6. USE AMPLE LIQUID

Adding enough liquid to the pot guarantees even cooking. Don't feel limited to using only water, though. Try experimenting with broth, wine, and other liquids.

CURRIED
Three-Grain Salad

Quinoa (KEEN-wah) is not only high in fiber, but also higher in protein than any other grain. Millet, usually found in health-food stores, is a tiny, delicate grain that is also rich in protein.

PREP: 13 MINUTES   **UNDER PRESSURE:** 5 MINUTES   **TOTAL:** 30 MINUTES

Cooking spray
¼ cup minced fresh onion
1 cup uncooked basmati rice
½ cup uncooked millet
½ cup uncooked quinoa
2 cups water
1 cup fat-free, lower-sodium chicken broth
½ cup raisins
½ cup sliced green onions
½ cup chopped red bell pepper
⅓ cup olive oil
2 tablespoons fresh lemon juice
2 teaspoons curry powder
½ teaspoon salt
¼ cup minced fresh cilantro

1 Heat a 6-quart pressure cooker over medium-high heat; coat cooker with cooking spray. Add onion; sauté 1 minute. Add rice, millet, and quinoa; sauté 30 seconds. Stir in 2 cups water and broth. Close lid securely; bring to high pressure over medium-high heat (about 4 minutes). Adjust heat to low or level needed to maintain high pressure; cook 5 minutes. Remove from heat; place cooker under cold running water. Let stand 7 minutes; remove lid. Fluff mixture with a fork. Spoon mixture into a large bowl; cool 5 minutes. Stir in raisins, green onions, and bell pepper.

2 Combine oil and next 3 ingredients (through salt) in a bowl; stir with a whisk. Pour oil mixture over rice mixture, tossing to coat. Stir in cilantro.

SERVES 7 (SERVING SIZE: ABOUT 1 CUP)
CALORIES 212; **FAT** 3.6G (SAT 0.5G, MONO 1.0G, POLY 1.7G); **PROTEIN** 4G; **CARB** 43G; **FIBER** 3G; **CHOL** 3MG; **IRON** 3MG; **SODIUM** 207MG; **CALC** 30MG

PRESSURE PERFECT TIP:
Allow the grains to cool before adding the dressing; it will coat the grains rather than being absorbed by them.

13 MINUTE PREP!

Cherry, Chicken, and Pecan
WHEAT BERRY SALAD

PREP: 13 MINUTES   UNDER PRESSURE: 18 MINUTES   TOTAL: 45 MINUTES

4½ cups water
1½ cups uncooked wheat berries
1 tablespoon canola oil
3 tablespoons olive oil, divided
2 tablespoons apple cider vinegar
¾ teaspoon kosher salt
½ teaspoon freshly ground black pepper
¼ teaspoon sugar

¼ cup pecan halves and pieces, toasted
6 ounces shredded skinless, boneless chicken breast
½ cup chopped onion
1 tablespoon chopped fresh thyme
1 cup fresh cherries, pitted and halved
1 ounce baby arugula leaves
2 ounces goat cheese, crumbled

1 Place 4½ cups water, wheat berries, and 1 tablespoon canola oil in a 6-quart pressure cooker. Close lid securely; bring to high pressure over high heat (about 4 minutes). Adjust heat to medium or level needed to maintain pressure; cook 18 minutes. Remove from heat; place cooker under running water. Let stand 7 minutes; remove lid. Fluff wheat berries with a fork.

2 Combine 2½ tablespoons olive oil, vinegar, salt, pepper, and sugar in a large bowl, stirring well with a whisk. Add wheat berries, nuts, and chicken; toss.

3 Heat a medium nonstick skillet over medium heat. Add 1½ teaspoons olive oil to pan; swirl to coat. Add onion and thyme; cook 3 minutes or until tender. Add to wheat berry mixture; toss. Stir in cherries and arugula; toss. Sprinkle with cheese.

SERVES 4 (SERVING SIZE: ABOUT 1¼ CUPS)
CALORIES 397; **FAT** 20.1G (SAT 4.4G, MONO 12G, POLY 2.8G); **PROTEIN** 21G; **CARB** 37G; **FIBER** 7G; **CHOL** 44MG; **IRON** 1MG; **SODIUM** 570MG; **CALC** 49MG

SMOKED SALMON
and Wheat Berry Salad

PREP: 10 MINUTES   UNDER PRESSURE: 18 MINUTES   TOTAL: 35 MINUTES

4½ cups water

1½ cups uncooked wheat berries

3 tablespoons olive oil, divided

1½ cups diced Fuji apple

½ cup vertically sliced red onion

½ cup chopped walnuts, toasted

4 ounces smoked salmon, cut into 1-inch pieces

2 medium celery stalks, thinly sliced

1 teaspoon grated lemon rind

2 tablespoons fresh lemon juice

1 tablespoon Dijon mustard

½ teaspoon kosher salt

½ teaspoon freshly ground black pepper

1 Place 4½ cups water, wheat berries, and 1 tablespoon olive oil in a 6-quart pressure cooker. Close lid securely; bring to high pressure over high heat. Adjust heat to medium or level needed to maintain pressure; cook 18 minutes. Remove from heat; place cooker under running water. Let stand 7 minutes; remove lid. Fluff wheat berries with a fork.

2 Combine wheat berries, apple, and next 4 ingredients (through celery) in a large bowl. Combine remaining olive oil and remaining ingredients in a small bowl, stirring with a whisk. Drizzle dressing over wheat berry mixture; toss to coat.

SERVES 4 (SERVING SIZE: 1½ CUPS)
CALORIES 389; **FAT** 18.7G (SAT 2.1G, MONO 6.8G, POLY 7.9G); **PROTEIN** 14G; **CARB** 45G; **FIBER** 9G; **CHOL** 7MG; **IRON** 3MG; **SODIUM** 570MG; **CALC** 54MG

Vegetable
YELLOW RICE

Finely chop the bell pepper and onion so they'll cook quickly.
To save time, choose frozen corn kernels over fresh.

PREP: 10 MINUTES **UNDER PRESSURE:** 3 MINUTES **TOTAL:** 26 MINUTES

½ cup water
1 (14.5-ounce) can fat-free, lower-sodium chicken broth
1 tablespoon olive oil
½ cup finely chopped onion
1 cup uncooked Arborio rice or other medium-grain rice
⅛ teaspoon powdered saffron (optional)
1 cup fresh corn kernels (about 2 ears)
1 cup finely chopped zucchini
½ cup finely chopped red bell pepper
1.3 ounces grated fresh Parmesan cheese (about ⅓ cup)
¼ teaspoon salt

1 Combine ½ cup water and broth in a medium saucepan. Bring to a simmer over medium-high heat; keep warm.

2 Heat a 6-quart pressure cooker over medium heat. Add oil to cooker; swirl to coat. Add onion; sauté 2 minutes. Add rice and saffron, if desired; sauté 30 seconds. Stir in broth mixture. Close lid securely; bring to high pressure over high heat (about 3 minutes). Adjust heat to medium or level needed to maintain high pressure; cook 3 minutes. Remove from heat; let stand 10 minutes. Place cooker under cold running water. Remove lid; stir in corn, zucchini, and bell pepper. Cook, uncovered, 3 minutes, stirring constantly. Remove from heat; stir in cheese and salt.

SERVES 9 (SERVING SIZE: ABOUT ½ CUP)
CALORIES 156; **FAT** 9.4G (SAT 1.7G, MONO 4.4G, POLY 1.3G); **PROTEIN** 11G; **CARB** 31G; **FIBER** 8G; **CHOL** 0MG; **IRON** 6MG; **SODIUM** 310MG; **CALC** 102MG

**SWAP
IN A SNAP:**
Saffron is a delicious,
but expensive, spice. For
a more economical dish,
use turmeric instead.

RISOTTO
with Tomato Topping

PREP: 10 MINUTES **UNDER PRESSURE:** 6 MINUTES **TOTAL:** 35 MINUTES

TOPPING:

1½ cups chopped seeded tomato
2 tablespoons chopped green
   onions
1½ teaspoons extra-virgin olive oil
1 teaspoon balsamic vinegar
¼ teaspoon crushed red pepper
⅛ teaspoon sugar
⅛ teaspoon salt
⅛ teaspoon freshly ground black
   pepper

RISOTTO:

2 tablespoons butter
1 cup chopped onion
1½ cups Arborio rice or other
   medium-grain rice
2 garlic cloves, minced
½ cup dry white wine
4 cups fat-free, lower-sodium
   chicken broth
½ teaspoon salt
¼ teaspoon freshly ground black
   pepper
⅛ teaspoon ground nutmeg
4 ounces grated fresh Parmesan
   cheese (about 1 cup)
⅓ cup finely chopped fresh basil
1 teaspoon grated lemon rind
2 tablespoons fresh lemon juice

1 To prepare topping, combine first 8 ingredients (through black pepper) in a bowl. Cover; let stand at room temperature.

2 To prepare risotto, melt butter in a 6-quart pressure cooker over medium heat; swirl to coat. Add onion; sauté 2 minutes. Add rice and garlic; cook 2 minutes, stirring constantly. Add wine; cook 1 minute or until liquid is absorbed, stirring frequently. Stir in broth and next 3 ingredients (through nutmeg). Close lid securely; bring to high pressure over high heat (about 4 minutes). Adjust heat to medium or level needed to maintain high pressure; cook 6 minutes. Remove from heat; place cooker under cold running water. Remove lid. Let stand 10 minutes. Stir in cheese and next 3 ingredients (through lemon juice). Serve risotto with tomato topping.

SERVES 10 (SERVING SIZE: ½ CUP RISOTTO AND ABOUT 1½ TABLESPOONS TOPPING)
CALORIES 200; **FAT** 7G (SAT 3.5G, MONO 0.6G, POLY 0.9G); **PROTEIN** 7G; **CARB** 27G; **FIBER** 2G; **CHOL** 15MG; **IRON** 0MG; **SODIUM** 490MG; **CALC** 132MG

PRESSURE PERFECT TIP:
Don't worry if the rice is a tad runny after cooking—it thickens as it stands.

PARMESAN RISOTTO

The pressure cooker creates creamy risotto in a hands-free way. Throw the ingredients in the pot, and 25 minutes later you'll have a risotto cooked to perfection.

PREP: 10 MINUTES **UNDER PRESSURE:** 8 MINUTES **TOTAL:** 25 MINUTES

1½ tablespoons butter

⅔ cup finely chopped shallots

3 garlic cloves, minced

1⅓ cups uncooked medium-grain rice

1 cup dry white wine, divided

3 cups fat-free, lower-sodium chicken broth

2 ounces fresh Parmigiano-Reggiano cheese, divided

1 teaspoon thyme leaves

½ teaspoon grated lemon rind

¼ teaspoon freshly ground black pepper

1 Melt butter in a 6-quart pressure cooker over medium-high heat; swirl to coat. Add shallots; sauté 2 minutes. Add garlic; sauté 30 seconds. Add rice; cook 1 minute, stirring constantly. Add ½ cup wine; cook 1 minute or until liquid is absorbed, stirring constantly. Stir in broth and ½ cup wine. Close lid securely; bring to high pressure over high heat (about 4 minutes). Adjust heat to medium or level needed to maintain high pressure; cook 8 minutes. Remove from heat; place cooker under cold running water. Remove lid.

2 Grate 1¾ ounces cheese; sprinkle grated cheese, thyme, lemon rind, and pepper over rice mixture. Let stand 4 minutes. Shave ¼ ounce cheese; top rice mixture with shaved cheese.

SERVES 9 (SERVING SIZE: ½ CUP)
CALORIES 179; **FAT** 3.1G (SAT 1.1G, MONO 0.7G, POLY 0.5G); **PROTEIN** 7.8G; **CARB** 32G; **FIBER** 6G; **CHOL** 4MG; **IRON** 2MG; **SODIUM** 307MG; **CALC** 66MG

SWAP IN A SNAP: Carnaroli or Arborio rice will work well in this dish.

FORK-TENDER MEATS

Spaghetti and Meatballs
WITH RED WINE

No more waiting hours for homemade meatballs! Have these on the table for dinner, even on a busy weeknight, in about 30 minutes.

PREP: 15 MINUTES **UNDER PRESSURE:** 5 MINUTES **TOTAL:** 30 MINUTES

1 pound extra-lean ground beef

²/₃ cup finely chopped onion, divided

½ cup panko (Japanese breadcrumbs)

1.5 ounces grated fresh Parmesan or Asiago cheese (about 6 tablespoons)

3 tablespoons oregano leaves, divided

1 garlic clove, minced and divided

1 teaspoon dried fennel seed

½ teaspoon crushed red pepper, divided

1 large egg, lightly beaten

1 tablespoon canola oil

½ cup dry red wine

2 teaspoons sugar

1 (28-ounce) can crushed tomatoes, undrained

12 ounces uncooked multigrain spaghetti (such as Barilla Plus)

Fresh oregano leaves (optional)

1 Combine beef, ⅓ cup onion, panko, cheese, 1½ tablespoons oregano, 1 teaspoon garlic, fennel seed, ¼ teaspoon crushed red pepper, and egg in a medium bowl. Shape mixture into 24 meatballs (about 1 tablespoon each).

2 Heat a 6-quart pressure cooker over medium heat. Add oil to cooker; swirl to coat. Add ⅓ cup onion and 1 teaspoon garlic; sauté 3 to 4 minutes or just until tender. Stir in wine, scraping cooker to loosen browned bits. Stir in 1½ tablespoons oregano, ¼ teaspoon crushed red pepper, and sugar. Arrange meatballs in a single layer in cooker; top with tomatoes (do not stir).

3 Close lid securely; bring to high pressure over high heat (about 4 minutes). Adjust heat to medium or level to maintain high pressure; cook 5 minutes. Remove from heat; place cooker under cold running water. Remove lid.

4 While meatballs cook, cook spaghetti according to package directions, omitting salt and fat; drain. Serve meatballs and tomato sauce over spaghetti. Sprinkle with oregano leaves, if desired.

SERVES 6 (SERVING SIZE: ABOUT ¾ CUP SPAGHETTI, 4 MEATBALLS, AND ½ CUP TOMATO SAUCE)
CALORIES 470; **FAT** 11G (SAT 3.5G, MONO 3.4G, POLY 2G); **PROTEIN** 33G; **CARB** 54G; **FIBER** 7G; **CHOL** 85MG; **IRON** 6MG; **SODIUM** 430MG; **CALC** 186MG

Braised Beef SHORT RIBS

Finishing the ribs under the broiler gives these rich cuts an extra boost of crispy texture that enhances the flavor of the meat.

PREP: 15 MINUTES UNDER PRESSURE: 30 MINUTES TOTAL: 53 MINUTES

1.1 ounces all-purpose flour (about ¼ cup)
2½ pounds flanken-cut beef short ribs (¾ inch thick)
1 teaspoon kosher salt
½ teaspoon freshly ground black pepper
2 tablespoons olive oil
¾ cup diced onion
⅓ cup diced celery
⅓ cup diced carrot
¼ cup chopped leek
1 garlic clove, minced
10 black peppercorns
5 juniper berries
3 thyme sprigs
2 bay leaves
¾ cup hot water
2 tablespoons veal demi-glace
¼ cup dry red wine
Additional thyme sprigs (optional)

1 Weigh or lightly spoon flour into a dry measuring cup; level with a knife. Place flour in a shallow dish. Sprinkle beef with salt and pepper; dredge in flour. Heat a 6-quart pressure cooker over medium-high heat. Add 1 tablespoon oil to cooker; swirl to coat. Add half of beef to cooker; cook 6 minutes, browning on all sides. Remove beef from pan. Repeat with 1 tablespoon oil and remaining beef.

2 Add onion and next 3 ingredients (through leek) to cooker; sauté 5 minutes. Add garlic; sauté 1 minute. Place peppercorns and next 3 ingredients (through bay leaves) on a double layer of cheesecloth. Gather edges of cheesecloth together; tie securely. Place cheesecloth bag in cooker; return beef to cooker. Combine ¾ cup hot water and demi-glace in a small bowl, stirring well. Add demi-glace mixture and wine to cooker.

3 Close lid securely; bring to high pressure over high heat (about 3 minutes). Adjust heat to medium or level to maintain high pressure; cook 30 minutes. Remove from heat; place cooker under cold running water. Remove lid. Remove ribs from cooker. Strain cooking liquid through a fine sieve into a bowl; discard solids. Skim fat off cooking liquid; discard fat.

4 Preheat broiler. Place ribs on a broiler pan. Broil 5 to 6 minutes or until edges are browned and crisp. Serve ribs with cooking liquid. Garnish with additional thyme sprigs, if desired.

SERVES 7 (SERVING SIZE: 1 SHORT RIB AND ABOUT 1 TABLESPOON COOKING LIQUID)
CALORIES 190; FAT 11G (SAT 3.5G, MONO 5.7G, POLY 0.8G); PROTEIN 14G; CARB 7G; FIBER 1G; CHOL 40MG; IRON 2MG; SODIUM 460MG; CALC 19MG

Cabernet-Braised
BEEF SHORT RIBS

Cooking short ribs in red wine will deliver an unbelievably rich sauce perfect for spooning over noodles. Serve with a chunk of bread to soak up all the sauce.

PREP: 10 MINUTES **UNDER PRESSURE:** 45 MINUTES **TOTAL:** 60 MINUTES

1 tablespoon olive oil
4 tablespoons all-purpose flour, divided
2 pounds bone-in beef short ribs, trimmed
½ teaspoon salt
½ teaspoon freshly ground black pepper
1½ cups (1-inch-thick) sliced celery
1 cup (1-inch-thick) sliced carrot
6 garlic cloves, sliced
2 (6-inch) rosemary sprigs
1 medium onion, cut into 8 wedges
2 tablespoons tomato paste
½ cup fat-free, lower-sodium beef broth
½ cup cabernet sauvignon or other dry red wine
¼ cup water
1 tablespoon cold water
3 cups hot cooked wide egg noodles
Chopped fresh parsley (optional)

1 Heat a 6-quart pressure cooker over medium-high heat. Add oil to cooker; swirl to coat. Place 3 tablespoons flour in a shallow dish. Sprinkle beef with salt and pepper; dredge in flour. Add beef to cooker; cook 8 minutes, browning on all sides. Remove beef from cooker, reserving 1 tablespoon drippings in cooker.

2 Add celery and next 4 ingredients (through onion) to drippings in cooker; sauté 4 minutes. Stir in tomato paste. Add broth, wine, and ¼ cup water to cooker, scraping cooker to loosen browned bits. Return ribs to pressure cooker. Close lid securely; bring to high pressure over high heat (about 4 minutes). Adjust heat to medium or level to maintain high pressure; cook 45 minutes. Remove from heat; place cooker under cold running water. Remove lid. Remove beef from pan. Strain cooking liquid through a fine sieve into a bowl; discard solids.

3 Return cooking liquid to cooker; bring to a boil over medium-high heat. Combine 1 tablespoon cold water and 1 tablespoon flour in a small bowl. Add flour mixture to cooking liquid, stirring with a whisk. Reduce heat, and simmer 3 minutes or until slightly thick, stirring constantly. Serve ribs and noodles with sauce. Garnish with chopped parsley, if desired.

SERVES 6 (SERVING SIZE: ½ CUP NOODLES, 1 SHORT RIB, AND ABOUT ¼ CUP SAUCE)
CALORIES 230; **FAT** 8G (SAT 2.5G, MONO 3.6G, POLY 0.8G); **PROTEIN** 13G;
CARB 23G; **FIBER** 2G; **CHOL** 45MG; **IRON** 2MG; **SODIUM** 250MG; **CALC** 32MG

DARK BEAN and BEEF CHILI

This serves a crowd, so invite friends who are hearty eaters. Serve warm corn bread on the side.

PREP: 15 MINUTES   **UNDER PRESSURE:** 20 MINUTES   **TOTAL:** 1 HOUR 30 MINUTES

1½ tablespoons canola oil

2 pounds chuck roast, trimmed and cut into 1-inch cubes

2 cups diced onion

2⅓ cups frozen fire-roasted corn kernels

2 cups diced green bell pepper (about 2 large)

2 cups lower-sodium beef broth

¼ cup chili powder

1 tablespoon ground cumin

2 teaspoons instant coffee granules

¼ teaspoon salt

2 (15-ounce) cans unsalted dark red kidney beans, rinsed and drained

2 (14.5-ounce) cans stewed tomatoes, undrained and chopped

1 cup light sour cream

Additional ground cumin (optional)

1 Heat a 6-quart pressure cooker over medium-high heat. Add 1½ teaspoons oil to cooker; swirl to coat. Add one-third of beef; cook 4 minutes, browning on all sides. Remove beef with a slotted spoon. Repeat procedure twice with remaining oil and beef. Add onion to cooker; sauté 3 minutes. Stir in corn and next 8 ingredients (through tomatoes). Return beef to pressure cooker.

2 Close lid securely; bring to high pressure over high heat (about 12 minutes). Adjust heat to medium or level to maintain high pressure; cook 20 minutes. Remove from heat; let stand 20 minutes or until pressure releases. Remove lid. Bring beef mixture to a simmer over medium-high heat; simmer 20 minutes or until slightly thick, stirring occasionally.

3 Serve chili with sour cream, and sprinkle with additional cumin, if desired.

SERVES 8 (SERVING SIZE: 1½ CUPS CHILI AND 2 TABLESPOONS SOUR CREAM)
CALORIES 430; **FAT** 8G (SAT 2.5G, MONO 3G, POLY 1.1G); **PROTEIN** 30G;
CARB 58G; **FIBER** 4G; **CHOL** 85MG; **IRON** 5MG; **SODIUM** 570MG; **CALC** 45MG

PRESSURE PERFECT TIP: Cut the beef in uniform pieces so they cook evenly.

BEEF BOURGUIGNONNE

This classic French stew is perfect cold-weather fare and is delicious over noodles or mashed potatoes.

PREP: 10 MINUTES **UNDER PRESSURE:** 20 MINUTES **TOTAL:** 46 MINUTES

1.1 ounces all-purpose flour (about ¼ cup)

½ teaspoon salt

½ teaspoon freshly ground black pepper

1½ pounds boneless chuck roast, trimmed and cut into 1-inch cubes

2 bacon slices, diced

½ cup dry red wine

1 (10½-ounce) can beef broth

3 cups baby carrots (about ¾ pound)

2 cups sliced shiitake mushroom caps (about ½ pound)

2 teaspoons dried thyme

6 shallots, halved (about ½ pound)

4 garlic cloves, thinly sliced

7 cups hot cooked medium egg noodles (about 5 cups uncooked pasta)

Fresh thyme leaves (optional)

1 Weigh or lightly spoon flour into a dry measuring cup; level with a knife. Combine flour, salt, and pepper in a large zip-top plastic bag. Add beef; seal and shake to coat.

2 Cook bacon in a 6-quart pressure cooker over medium heat 30 seconds. Add half of beef mixture to cooker; cook 5 minutes, browning on all sides. Remove beef and bacon from cooker. Repeat procedure with remaining beef mixture. Return cooked beef and bacon to cooker. Stir in wine and broth, scraping pan to loosen browned bits. Add carrots and next 4 ingredients (through garlic). Close lid securely; bring to high pressure over high heat (about 6 minutes). Adjust heat to medium or level needed to maintain high pressure; cook 20 minutes. Remove from heat; place cooker under cold running water. Remove lid. Serve beef mixture over noodles. Garnish with thyme leaves, if desired.

SERVES 7 (SERVING SIZE: 1 CUP BEEF MIXTURE AND 1 CUP NOODLES)
CALORIES 376; **FAT** 12.5G (SAT 4.5G, MONO 5.4G, POLY 1.3G); **PROTEIN** 25G; **CARB** 41G; **FIBER** 3G; **CHOL** 44MG; **IRON** 5MG; **SODIUM** 525MG; **CALC** 3MG

SWAP IN A SNAP: Portobello mushrooms make a good substitute for the shiitake variety.

Vegetable
BEEF SOUP

To quickly remove the tough stems from the kale, fold the leaves in half along the rib. Cut the leaves away from the rib with a paring knife. Stack the leaves, and slice into pieces.

PREP: 25 MINUTES   **UNDER PRESSURE:** 12 MINUTES   **TOTAL:** 52 MINUTES

1 tablespoon olive oil
½ pound boneless chuck roast, trimmed and cut into ½-inch cubes
1½ cups chopped onion
1¼ cups sliced carrot
1 cup chopped celery
1 cup dried navy beans
4 cups lower-sodium beef broth
3 cups water
½ cup uncooked pearl barley
1 teaspoon thyme leaves
¼ teaspoon salt
1 (14.5-ounce) can diced tomatoes with basil, garlic, and oregano, undrained
4 cups thinly sliced kale
1 teaspoon thyme leaves
1 teaspoon balsamic vinegar
6 teaspoons shredded fresh Parmesan cheese

1 Heat a 6-quart pressure cooker over medium-high heat. Add oil to cooker; swirl to coat. Add beef; cook 2 to 3 minutes or until browned, stirring frequently. Add onion, carrot, and celery; cook 4 minutes or until vegetables are lightly browned, stirring frequently. Stir in beans and next 6 ingredients (through tomatoes).

2 Close lid securely; bring to high pressure over medium-high heat (about 8 minutes). Adjust heat to medium or level to maintain high pressure; cook 12 minutes. Remove from heat; let stand 15 minutes or until pressure releases. Remove lid. Add kale, thyme, and vinegar, stirring until kale wilts. Divide soup among 12 bowls; sprinkle with cheese.

SERVES 12 (SERVING SIZE: 1 CUP SOUP AND ½ TEASPOON CHEESE)
CALORIES 150; **FAT** 1.5G (SAT 0.5G, MONO 0.4G, POLY 0.3G); **PROTEIN** 11G; **CARB** 24G; **FIBER** 8G; **CHOL** 10MG; **IRON** 2MG; **SODIUM** 280MG; **CALC** 105MG

SWAP IN A SNAP: Use any green such as spinach, chard, or collards in place of the kale.

POT ROAST
with Vegetables

Pot roast is the go-to recipe for an easy, comforting meal. Leftover meat and gravy make great hot roast beef sandwiches the next day.

PREP: 15 MINUTES **UNDER PRESSURE:** 45 MINUTES **TOTAL:** 1 HOUR 22 MINUTES

2 tablespoons canola oil
1 (3-pound) boneless chuck roast, trimmed
1 cup minced onion
3 cups water
1 cup dry red wine
1 teaspoon sugar
1 teaspoon hot sauce
¾ teaspoon salt
2½ pounds small red potatoes, halved
4 carrots, peeled and cut into 1-inch slices
1 (10.5-ounce) can beef broth
1 (8-ounce) can tomato sauce
Chopped fresh parsley (optional)

1 Heat an 8-quart pressure cooker over medium-high heat. Add oil to cooker; swirl to coat. Add roast to cooker; cook 6 minutes, browning on all sides. Add onion and remaining ingredients. Close lid securely; bring to high pressure over high heat (about 5 minutes). Adjust heat to medium or level needed to maintain high pressure; cook 45 minutes. Remove from heat; place cooker under cold running water. Remove lid.

2 Remove roast and vegetables with a slotted spoon; keep warm. Bring broth mixture to a boil over medium-high heat; cook until reduced to 5 cups (about 20 minutes). Cut roast across grain into thin slices. Serve roast with vegetable mixture and cooking liquid. Garnish with parsley, if desired.

SERVES 8 (SERVING SIZE: 4 OUNCES ROAST, ABOUT ½ CUP VEGETABLES, AND ABOUT ½ CUP COOKING LIQUID)
CALORIES 390; **FAT** 10G (SAT 3G, MONO 4.3G, POLY 1.9G); **PROTEIN** 37G; **CARB** 31G; **FIBER** 4G; **CHOL** 65MG; **IRON** 4MG; **SODIUM** 730MG; **CALC** 47MG

PRESSURE PERFECT TIP:
Cut the potatoes and carrots in uniform pieces so they'll cook evenly.

KALAMATA and SUN-DRIED TOMATO BRISKET

Try this saucy beef over pasta, rice, or potatoes, or on top of crusty Italian whole-grain bread slices for open-faced sandwiches.

PREP: 15 MINUTES **UNDER PRESSURE:** 45 MINUTES **TOTAL:** 1 HOUR 30 MINUTES

2 teaspoons canola oil
1 (2½-pound) beef brisket, trimmed and cut in half
8 medium shallots, peeled and halved
2 cups dry red wine
1½ tablespoons Worcestershire sauce
1 (8-ounce) can tomato sauce
⅓ cup thinly sliced sun-dried tomato halves
1 teaspoon dried oregano
1 teaspoon garlic powder
½ cup chopped pitted kalamata olives
¼ teaspoon salt
Chopped fresh parsley (optional)

1 Heat a 6-quart pressure cooker over medium-high heat. Add 1 teaspoon oil to cooker; swirl to coat. Add half of brisket to cooker; cook 2 minutes on each side or until browned. Remove from cooker. Repeat procedure with 1 teaspoon oil and remaining brisket half. Add shallots to drippings in cooker; sauté 2 minutes or until lightly browned. Stir in wine, Worcestershire sauce, and tomato sauce. Add brisket halves and any accumulated juices, sun-dried tomatoes, oregano, and garlic powder.

2 Close lid securely; bring to high pressure over high heat (about 8 minutes). Adjust heat to medium or level to maintain high pressure; cook 45 minutes. Remove from heat; let stand 10 minutes or until pressure releases. Remove lid. Remove brisket from cooker; let stand 5 minutes. Cut brisket diagonally across grain into thin slices. Add olives and salt to cooking liquid in cooker. Spoon cooking liquid over brisket before serving; sprinkle with parsley, if desired.

SERVES 8 (SERVING SIZE: 4 OUNCES BRISKET AND ABOUT ⅓ CUP SAUCE)
CALORIES 340; **FAT** 14G (SAT 4G, MONO 7.4G, POLY 1G); **PROTEIN** 31G;
CARB 9G; **FIBER** 1G; **CHOL** 90MG; **IRON** 4MG; **SODIUM** 510MG; **CALC** 28MG

SWAP IN A SNAP: Quarter one red onion, and use in place of the shallots.

QUICKER MEATS!

Here's how to cook your favorite cuts of beef, pork, or lamb 2 times faster than the 3 to 4 hours using traditional oven and stovetop methods.

START HERE!

1. Sprinkle cuts of meat with salt, pepper, and desired seasonings. Add 1 tablespoon oil to a 6-quart pressure cooker; swirl to coat. Brown cuts according to the chart. Add 2 cups of desired liquid.

2. Close lid securely; bring to high pressure over high heat (5 to 12 minutes), and maintain pressure according to chart.

3. Remove from heat, and let stand until pressure has released. Remove lid. If needed, simmer meat on stovetop until liquid is thickened to desired consistency.

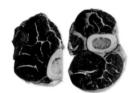

BEEF SHANK

TOTAL TIME: 1 HOUR 20 MINUTES

In batches, cook 6 (8-ounce) beef shanks 6 minutes, turning to brown all sides. Add liquid, and cook under pressure 45 minutes.

CHUCK ROAST

TOTAL TIME: 60 MINUTES

Cook 1 (3- to 4-pound) chuck roast 6 minutes, turning to brown all sides. Add liquid, and cook under pressure 25 minutes.

BRISKET

TOTAL TIME: 1 HOUR 56 MINUTES

Cook 1 (2- to 4-pound) brisket; cook 6 minutes, turning to brown all sides. Add liquid, and cook under pressure 1 hour and 30 minutes.

SIRLOIN TOP ROAST

TOTAL TIME: 56 MINUTES

Cook 1 (3-pound) sirloin top roast 6 minutes, turning to brown all sides. Add liquid, and cook under pressure 20 minutes.

PORK RIBS

TOTAL TIME: 56 MINUTES

Cook 1 (3-pound) rack of pork ribs 6 minutes, turning to brown all sides. Add liquid, and cook under pressure 20 minutes.

PORK SHOULDER

TOTAL TIME: 1 HOUR 56 MINUTES

Cook 1 (4-pound) pork shoulder 6 minutes, turning to brown all sides. Add liquid, and cook under pressure 1 hour and 30 minutes.

LAMB SHANK

TOTAL TIME: 1 HOUR 20 MINUTES

In batches, cook 6 (6-ounce) lamb shanks 6 minutes, turning to brown all sides. Add liquid, and cook under pressure 45 minutes.

BEEFY BORSCHT
with Dill Cream

PREP: 15 MINUTES   UNDER PRESSURE: 52 MINUTES   TOTAL: 1 HOUR 30 MINUTES

DILL CREAM:
½ cup heavy whipping cream
6 dill sprigs

SOUP:
Cooking spray
2¼ pounds cross-cut beef shanks
7 cups lower-sodium beef broth
1 tablespoon canola oil
2 cups chopped onion
4 garlic cloves, crushed
2 tablespoons tomato paste
4 cups thinly sliced red cabbage
3 cups coarsely chopped peeled red beets (about 1½ pounds)
1½ cups chopped peeled celeriac (celery root)
1 cup chopped carrot
12 ounces Yukon gold potatoes, coarsely chopped
3 tablespoons red wine vinegar
2 teaspoons kosher salt
¾ teaspoon freshly ground black pepper
Dill sprigs (optional)

1 To prepare dill cream, place whipping cream in a medium microwave-safe bowl. Microwave at HIGH 1 minute or until heated. Add dill; cover and chill.

2 To prepare soup, heat a 6-quart pressure cooker over medium-high heat. Coat pan with cooking spray. Add beef to pan; cook 4 minutes on each side or until well browned. Add broth. Close lid securely; bring to high pressure over high heat about 7 minutes. Adjust heat to medium or level needed to maintain high pressure; cook 45 minutes. Remove from heat; release pressure by placing cooker under cold running water. Remove lid. Strain broth through a colander over a large bowl. Place beef on a cutting board; discard remaining solids. Cool beef slightly. Shred meat; discard bones, fat, and gristle. Set meat aside.

3 Heat cooker over medium-high heat. Add oil; swirl to coat. Add chopped onion and garlic; sauté 3 minutes. Add tomato paste; sauté 1 minute. Add broth, cabbage, and next 4 ingredients (through potato). Close lid securely; bring to high pressure over high heat about 7 minutes. Adjust heat to medium or level needed to maintain high pressure; cook 7 minutes. Remove from heat; release pressure by placing cooker under cold running water. Remove lid. Stir in beef, vinegar, 2 teaspoons salt, and pepper.

4 Remove cream from refrigerator; discard dill. Beat cream with a mixer at high speed until soft peaks form. Spoon over soup; garnish with dill, if desired.

SERVES 12 (SERVING SIZE: ABOUT 1⅓ CUPS SOUP AND 2 TEASPOONS CREAM)
CALORIES 224; **FAT** 10.7G (SAT 4.6G, MONO 4.3G, POLY 0.8G); **PROTEIN** 14G; **CARB** 18G; **FIBER** 4G; **CHOL** 38MG; **IRON** 2G; **SODIUM** 503MG; **CALC** 62MG

Braised
LAMB SHANKS

Succulent lamb shanks cook to perfection
in a homemade tomato sauce.

PREP: 35 MINUTES   UNDER PRESSURE: 45 MINUTES   TOTAL: 1 HOUR 30 MINUTES

2 tablespoons olive oil
4 (1-pound) lamb shanks
1 cup chopped onion
¼ cup diced carrot
2 tablespoons diced celery
2 garlic cloves, minced
½ cup dry red wine
¼ cup chopped fresh basil
1 tablespoon chopped fresh
  oregano
2 teaspoons unsalted tomato
  paste
½ teaspoon salt
⅛ teaspoon freshly ground
  black pepper
1/16 teaspoon crushed red pepper
2 (26.46-ounce) boxes chopped
  tomatoes (such as Pomì)
¼ cup chopped pitted kalamata
  olives (about 13 olives)

1 Heat a 6-quart pressure cooker over medium heat. Add 1 table-spoon oil to cooker; swirl to coat. Add 2 lamb shanks to cooker; cook 5 minutes, browning on all sides. Remove lamb from cooker. Repeat procedure with 1 tablespoon oil and 2 lamb shanks. Add onion and next 3 ingredients (through garlic) to cooker; sauté 3 minutes. Stir in wine, scraping cooker to loosen browned bits. Add basil and next 6 ingredients (through tomatoes). Bring to a simmer; cook 12 minutes, stirring occasionally.

2 Return lamb to cooker. Close lid securely; bring to high pressure over high heat (about 7 minutes). Adjust heat to medium or level to maintain high pressure; cook 45 minutes. Remove from heat; place cooker under cold running water. Remove lid. Remove lamb from pan. Stir olives into vegetable mixture in cooker. Bring to a boil over medium-high heat; reduce heat, and simmer 10 minutes or until slightly thick. Serve lamb shanks with vegetable mixture.

SERVES 4 (SERVING SIZE: 1 LAMB SHANK AND ABOUT 1 CUP VEGETABLE MIXTURE)
CALORIES 450; **FAT** 16G (SAT 3.5G, MONO 10G, POLY 1.9G); **PROTEIN** 43G;
CARB 25G; **FIBER** 4G; **CHOL** 130MG; **IRON** 6MG; **SODIUM** 690MG; **CALC** 97MG

PRESSURE PERFECT TIP:
Brown the lamb shanks in the pressure cooker before cooking under pressure to enhance the flavor of the dish.

TUSCAN LAMB SHANKS

Rosemary, a perfect partner for lamb, nicely compliments the Great Northern beans. Try it served over polenta or egg noodles.

PREP: 35 MINUTES **UNDER PRESSURE:** 45 MINUTES **TOTAL:** 1 HOUR 37 MINUTES

¾ cup dried Great Northern beans
3¼ cups water, divided
3 pounds lamb shanks (about 2 large shanks)
2 tablespoons all-purpose flour
½ teaspoon salt
½ teaspoon freshly ground black pepper
2 teaspoons olive oil, divided
½ cup sliced shallots
6 garlic cloves, sliced
1 cup dry red wine
¼ cup sun-dried tomato sprinkles
1 tablespoon chopped fresh or 1 teaspoon dried rosemary
1 tablespoon Worcestershire sauce
1 (14¼-ounce) can lower-sodium beef broth

1 Sort and wash beans; combine beans and 3 cups water in a small saucepan. Bring to a boil; cook 1 minute. Remove from heat. Let stand 20 minutes. Drain; set aside.

2 Trim fat from lamb. Place flour, salt, and pepper in a large zip-top plastic bag; add lamb. Seal; shake to coat. Remove lamb from bag; shake off excess flour mixture. Reserve 1½ teaspoons flour mixture, and set aside.

3 Heat a 6-quart pressure cooker over medium heat. Add 1 teaspoon oil to cooker; swirl to coat. Add 1 lamb shank; cook 8 minutes on all sides or until browned. Remove lamb from pan. Repeat procedure with 1 teaspoon oil and 1 lamb shank. Return lamb to pressure cooker. Add shallots and garlic, and sauté 2 minutes. Add beans, ¼ cup water, reserved 1½ teaspoons flour mixture, red wine, and next 4 ingredients (through broth).

4 Close lid; bring to high pressure over high heat (about 7 minutes). Adjust heat to medium or level needed to maintain high pressure; cook 45 minutes. Remove from heat; place cooker under cold running water. Remove lid. Remove lamb from pan; cool completely.

5 Remove meat from bones; discard bones, fat, and gristle. Skim fat from surface. Stir meat into bean mixture.

SERVES 5 (SERVING SIZE: 1 CUP STEW)
CALORIES 450; **FAT** 9G (SAT 2.5G, MONO 4G, POLY 1.2G); **PROTEIN** 37G;
CARB 46G; **FIBER** 7G; **CHOL** 105MG; **IRON** 6G; **SODIUM** 370MG; **CALC** 99MG

Jalapeño-Glazed
PORK CHOPS AND RICE

Jalapeño jelly makes a quick glaze for any type of meat.
The heat will vary depending on the brand.

PREP: 25 MINUTES   **UNDER PRESSURE:** 20 MINUTES   **TOTAL:** 48 MINUTES

6 (8-ounce) bone-in pork chops
(about ³/₄ inch thick)
¹/₂ teaspoon salt, divided
¹/₂ teaspoon freshly ground
black pepper, divided
1 tablespoon canola oil
2 cups uncooked brown
basmati rice
1 cup chopped onion
2 garlic cloves, chopped
2¹/₂ cups water
2 cups fat-free, lower-sodium
chicken broth
¹/₂ cup jalapeño pepper jelly
¹/₄ cup sliced green onions

1 Sprinkle pork chops with ¼ teaspoon salt and ¼ teaspoon pepper. Heat a 6-quart pressure cooker over medium-high heat. Add 1 teaspoon oil to cooker; swirl to coat. Add 2 pork chops to cooker; cook 1 minute on each side or until browned. Remove pork from cooker; set aside. Repeat procedure twice with remaining pork chops. Reduce heat to medium. Add 2 teaspoons oil to cooker. Add rice, onion, and garlic; sauté 3 minutes or until onion is tender. Stir in ¼ teaspoon salt, ¼ teaspoon pepper, 2½ cups water, and broth.

2 Close lid securely; bring to high pressure over high heat (about 3 minutes). Adjust heat to medium-high or level to maintain high pressure; cook 17 minutes. Remove from heat; place cooker under cold running water. Remove lid. Add pork chops to cooker. Close lid securely; bring to high pressure over high heat (about 7 minutes). Adjust heat to low or level to maintain high pressure, cook 3 minutes. Remove from heat; place cooker under cold running water. Remove lid.

3 Remove pork chops from cooker. Place rice mixture on a serving platter; top with pork chops. Place jelly in a small microwave-safe bowl. Microwave at HIGH 30 to 60 seconds or until jelly melts. Brush pork chops with warm jelly, and sprinkle with green onions.

SERVES 6 (SERVING SIZE: 1 PORK CHOP AND ³/₄ CUP RICE MIXTURE)
CALORIES 490; **FAT** 10G (SAT 2G, MONO 3.6G, POLY 1.3G); **PROTEIN** 39G;
CARB 61G; **FIBER** 3G; **CHOL** 10MG; **IRON** 2MG; **SODIUM** 470MG; **CALC** 40MG

**SWAP
IN A SNAP:**
For a sweeter sauce,
use orange marmalade
or fig preserves.

Sweet Heat-Packed
PORK RIBS

These tender ribs get a boost of sweet heat and smoky flavor from both dried and canned chipotle chiles.

PREP: 15 MINUTES **UNDER PRESSURE:** 20 MINUTES **TOTAL:** 65 MINUTES

2 teaspoons canola oil
²/₃ cup finely chopped onion
1 cup ketchup
1 cup bottled chili sauce
1 cup water
¼ cup cider vinegar
2½ tablespoons finely chopped chipotle chiles, canned in adobo sauce
½ teaspoon crushed red pepper
2 garlic cloves, minced
3 pounds baby back pork ribs (2 racks)
4 teaspoons chipotle chile powder
1½ teaspoons garlic powder
½ cup packed brown sugar

1 Heat a 6-quart pressure cooker over medium heat. Add oil to cooker; swirl to coat. Add onion; sauté 5 minutes or until tender. Stir in ketchup and next 6 ingredients (through garlic). Bring to a boil; reduce heat, and simmer 5 minutes, stirring occasionally. Remove ½ cup ketchup mixture from pressure cooker; set aside.

2 Remove membrane from bone sides of ribs. Cut ribs into 4 pieces to fit in cooker. Combine chile powder, and garlic powder in a small bowl. Rub meat sides of ribs with spice mixture. Place ribs in cooker. Spoon reserved ½ cup ketchup mixture over ribs. Close lid securely; bring to high pressure over high heat (about 6 minutes). Adjust heat to medium or level to maintain high pressure; cook 20 minutes. Remove from heat; let stand 11 minutes or until pressure releases. Remove lid. Transfer ribs to a foil-lined jell-roll pan or broiler pan, meat sides up, and set aside.

3 Skim fat from sauce in cooker; discard fat. Add brown sugar to sauce; bring to a boil. Reduce heat, and simmer, uncovered, 10 minutes or until slightly thick, stirring frequently. Reserve ½ cup reduced sauce.

4 Preheat broiler. Brush ribs with ½ cup sauce. Broil ribs 3 to 5 minutes or until browned and crispy.

SERVES 8 (SERVING SIZE: 2 RIBS)
CALORIES 350; **FAT** 17G (SAT 6G, MONO 7.5G, POLY 2.9G); **PROTEIN** 17G; **CARB** 33G; **FIBER** 1G; **CHOL** 60MG; **IRON** 1MG; **SODIUM** 750MG; **CALC** 75MG

Savory Pork and Vegetable
SUPPER

Pressure cooking pork in broth, dried herbs,
and spices infuses it with flavor and makes it tender.

PREP: 20 MINUTES   **UNDER PRESSURE:** 65 MINUTES   **TOTAL:** 1 HOUR 30 MINUTES

2 teaspoons Hungarian sweet
   paprika
1 teaspoon freshly ground black
   pepper
¾ teaspoon salt
½ teaspoon dried rubbed sage
½ teaspoon dried thyme
½ teaspoon dry mustard
3 pounds boneless pork
   shoulder (Boston butt),
   trimmed
1 tablespoon canola oil
2½ cups thinly sliced leek
   (about 2 large)
4 garlic cloves, minced
1 (14.5-ounce) can fat-free,
   lower-sodium chicken broth
2 cups (1-inch) sliced carrot
2 pounds red potatoes,
   quartered

1 Combine first 6 ingredients in a small bowl. Rub spice mixture over pork. Heat a 6-quart pressure cooker over medium-high heat. Add oil to cooker; swirl to coat. Add pork; cook 6 minutes, browning on all sides. Remove pork from pan; set aside.

2 Add leek and garlic to cooker; sauté 2 minutes. Add broth; bring to a simmer. Return pork to cooker; spoon leek mixture over pork. Close lid securely; bring to high pressure over high heat (about 3 minutes). Adjust heat to medium or level needed to maintain high pressure; cook 50 minutes. Remove from heat; place cooker under cold running water. Remove lid; stir in carrot and potato.

3 Close lid securely; bring to high pressure over high heat (about 4 minutes). Adjust heat to medium or level needed to maintain high pressure; cook 15 minutes. Remove from heat; place cooker under cold running water. Remove lid; remove vegetables and pork from pan with a slotted spoon. Cut pork across grain into ¼-inch-thick slices. Serve pork and vegetables with cooking liquid.

SERVES 6 (SERVING SIZE: ABOUT 4 OUNCES PORK, ABOUT ¾ CUP VEGETABLES, AND ¼ CUP COOKING LIQUID)
CALORIES 350; **FAT** 10G (SAT 3G, MONO 4.7G, POLY 1.7G); **PROTEIN** 29G; **CARB** 34G; **FIBER** 5G; **CHOL** 80MG; **IRON** 4MG; **SODIUM** 590MG; **CALC** 74MG

6 STEPS
to Perfectly Cooked
MEAT

A pressure cooker is a magical tool for transforming tough, inexpensive cuts of meat into a melt-in-your mouth dish. Follow these steps to guarantee a successful outcome.

1. CHOOSE THE RIGHT CUT

Select a cut of meat that is tough and has a lot of connective tissue. As it cooks, the connective tissue will break down and create tons of flavor.

2. CUT IN UNIFORM PIECES

If chunks of meat have been cut into varying sizes, they won't cook evenly, resulting in some pieces being tough and chewy.

3. SEASON

Adding seasonings to the meat prior to cooking enhances flavor. But be careful not to overdo it; the seasonings can burn on the bottom of the pot.

4. BROWN THE MEAT FIRST

Browning the meat with a little oil before adding pressure will develop the flavor of the dish.

5. BROWN THE AROMATICS SECOND

Don't brown the meat and aromatics at the same time. Start with the meat, and then set aside. Next, add the aromatics, and cook until brown.

6. USE AMPLE LIQUID

Add water or broth for even cooking. Liquid is needed for the pot to come to pressure. The amount used will impact the cooking time.

ROAST PORK
with Brussels Sprouts and Sweet Potatoes

PREP: 20 MINUTES   UNDER PRESSURE: 31 MINUTES   TOTAL: 1 HOUR 20 MINUTES

2½ pounds boneless pork shoulder (Boston butt), trimmed and cut into 4 pieces
1 teaspoon paprika
¾ teaspoon salt, divided
⅝ teaspoon freshly ground black pepper, divided
1 garlic clove, minced
1 tablespoon canola oil, divided
1 large onion, cut into 8 wedges
2 cups water
2 tablespoons chopped fresh tarragon
1½ pounds peeled sweet potatoes, cut into 2-inch pieces
1 pound Brussels sprouts, trimmed and halved
½ cup honey mustard

1 Pat pork dry with paper towels. Combine paprika, ½ teaspoon salt, ½ teaspoon pepper, and garlic in a small bowl. Sprinkle pork with spice mixture. Heat a 6-quart pressure cooker over high heat. Add 2 teaspoons oil to cooker; swirl to coat. Add pork to cooker; cook 8 minutes, browning on all sides. Remove pork from cooker; keep warm.

2 Heat 1 teaspoon oil in cooker; add onion, and sauté 3 minutes or until lightly browned. Stir in 2 cups water, scraping cooker to loosen browned bits. Place pork on top of onion; stir in tarragon.

3 Close lid securely; bring to high pressure over high heat (about 5 minutes). Adjust heat to medium or level to maintain high pressure; cook 28 minutes. Remove from heat; place cooker under cold running water. Remove lid. Remove pork, and set aside.

4 Add sweet potato and Brussels sprouts to onion mixture in cooker. Close lid securely; bring to high pressure over high heat (about 7 minutes). Adjust heat to medium or level to maintain high pressure; cook 3 minutes. Remove from heat; place cooker under cold running water. Remove lid. Remove vegetables with a slotted spoon; place on a serving platter, and sprinkle with ¼ teaspoon salt. Do not toss.

5 Shred pork into bite-sized pieces; place on platter with vegetables. Sprinkle pork with ⅛ teaspoon pepper. Serve pork and vegetables with honey mustard.

SERVES 8 (SERVING SIZE: 3 OUNCES PORK AND ¾ CUP VEGETABLES)
CALORIES 360; **FAT** 16G (SAT 5G, MONO 7.5G, POLY 1.9G); **PROTEIN** 27G; **CARB** 22G; **FIBER** 4G; **CHOL** 85MG; **IRON** 3; **SODIUM** 410MG; **CALC** 74MG

PORK CARNITAS TACOS

Pork shoulder, quick-braised with orange juice and spices in the pressure cooker, and then broiled to crispy perfection, provides the base for our Pork Carnitas Tacos. For a lower carb count, swap lettuce cups for the corn tortillas.

PREP: 25 MINUTES   UNDER PRESSURE: 25 MINUTES   TOTAL: 1 HOUR 30 MINUTES

1½ cups fresh orange juice
1 cup thinly sliced onion
5 teaspoons chipotle chile powder
1 tablespoon ground cumin
1 teaspoon kosher salt
6 garlic cloves, minced
3 pounds boneless pork shoulder (Boston butt), trimmed and cut into 2-inch pieces
14 (6-inch) corn tortillas
2½ cups chopped tomato
½ cup cilantro leaves
Lime wedges (optional)

1 Combine first 6 ingredients in a 6-quart pressure cooker. Add pork, tossing to coat. Close lid securely; bring to high pressure over high heat (about 15 minutes). Adjust heat to medium or level to maintain high pressure; cook 25 minutes. Remove from heat; let stand 15 minutes or until pressure releases. Remove lid. Remove pork from cooker with a slotted spoon; shred with 2 forks to measure 4¾ cups meat. Remove and discard any chunks of fat. Spread pork in a single layer on a jelly-roll pan or broiler pan lined with foil.

2 Skim fat from cooking liquid in cooker; discard fat. Bring cooking liquid to a boil. Reduce heat, and simmer 5 minutes or until slightly thick, stirring frequently.

3 Preheat broiler.

4 Drizzle pork with ¼ cup cooking liquid. Discard remaining cooking liquid, or set aside for serving, if desired. Broil pork 3 to 5 minutes or until pork is browned and edges are crispy, turning pork occasionally.

5 Heat tortillas in microwave according to package directions. Spoon ⅓ cup shredded pork mixture onto each tortilla. Top each with about 3 tablespoons tomato and about 1½ teaspoons cilantro. Serve with lime wedges, if desired.

SERVES 7 (SERVING SIZE: 2 TACOS)
CALORIES 230; **FAT** 5G (SAT 1.5G, MONO 1.9G, POLY 0.8G); **PROTEIN** 25G; **CARB** 21G; **FIBER** 3G; **CHOL** 70MG; **IRON** 1MG; **SODIUM** 310MG; **CALC** 31MG

PRESSURE PERFECT TIP:
Cut the pork into uniform pieces so that it cooks evenly.

CUMIN PORK
and Poblano Corn

PREP: 25 MINUTES   UNDER PRESSURE: 35 MINUTES   TOTAL: 1 HOUR 25 MINUTES

1 (2½-pound) bone-in pork shoulder, trimmed
1½ tablespoons chili powder
2 teaspoons ground cumin
½ teaspoon salt, divided
¾ teaspoon freshly ground black pepper
2 tablespoons extra-virgin olive oil, divided
1½ cups water
1⅓ cups fat-free, lower-sodium chicken broth
1 tablespoon minced fresh garlic
4 poblano chiles, seeded and chopped (about 3 cups)
1 large red bell pepper, diced (about 1½ cups)
4 cups fresh corn kernels (about 5 ears)
¾ cup chopped fresh cilantro
Lime wedges

1 Pat pork dry with paper towels. Combine chili powder, cumin, ¼ teaspoon salt, and black pepper in a medium bowl. Remove 1 tablespoon spice mixture; set aside. Add pork to remaining spice mixture in bowl, turning to coat. Heat a 6-quart pressure cooker over medium heat. Add 1 tablespoon oil to cooker; swirl to coat. Add pork to cooker; cook 4 minutes, browning on all sides. Remove pork from cooker; add 1½ cups water and broth, scraping cooker to loosen browned bits. Return pork to cooker.

2 Close lid securely; bring to high pressure over high heat (about 8 minutes). Adjust heat to medium or level to maintain high pressure; cook 35 minutes. Remove from heat; let stand 8 minutes or until pressure releases. Remove lid. Remove pork from cooker; separate pork into bite-sized pieces.

3 Strain cooking liquid through a fine sieve into a bowl; discard solids. Skim fat off cooking liquid; discard fat. Return skimmed liquid to cooker. Bring liquid to a boil over high heat. Cook until reduced to 2 cups (about 3 to 4 minutes). Pour sauce into a bowl; cover and keep warm.

4 Heat cooker over medium-high heat. Add 1 tablespoon oil; swirl to coat. Add reserved 1 tablespoon spice mixture, garlic, poblano chile, and bell pepper; sauté 5 minutes or until crisp-tender. Stir in corn; cover (do not lock) and cook 4 minutes or until thoroughly heated. Remove from heat; stir in ¼ teaspoon salt and cilantro. Divide vegetable mixture among 6 bowls. Top with pork and sauce; serve with lime wedges.

SERVES 6 (SERVING SIZE: ABOUT 1 CUP VEGETABLE MIXTURE, ⅔ CUP PORK, AND ⅓ CUP SAUCE)
CALORIES 330; **FAT** 13G (SAT 2.5G, MONO 5.8G, POLY 1.6G); **PROTEIN** 32G; **CARB** 25G; **FIBER** 4G; **CHOL** 80MG; **IRON** 3MG; **SODIUM** 510MG; **CALC** 41MG

SMOKY PORK
and Hominy Soup
Try this soup garnished with radish slices and sour cream.

PREP: 25 MINUTES **UNDER PRESSURE:** 35 MINUTES **TOTAL:** 1 HOUR 20 MINUTES

4 teaspoons canola oil
2¼ pounds boneless pork shoulder (Boston butt), trimmed and cut into 1-inch pieces
2 cups diced onion
1½ cups water
¼ cup tomato paste
2 tablespoons Spanish smoked paprika
1 tablespoon ground cumin
2 teaspoons dried oregano, crumbled
1½ teaspoons garlic powder
3 (14.5-ounce) cans fat-free, lower-sodium chicken broth
3 (15.5-ounce) cans white hominy, rinsed and drained
1 cup chopped fresh cilantro

1 Heat a 6-quart pressure cooker over medium-high heat. Add 2 teaspoons oil to cooker; swirl to coat. Add half of pork to pan; cook 6 minutes, browning on all sides. Remove pork with a slotted spoon; keep warm. Repeat procedure with 2 teaspoons oil and remaining pork. Return cooked pork to pan; stir in onion and next 7 ingredients (through broth).

2 Close lid securely; bring to high pressure over high heat (about 8 minutes). Reduce heat to medium or level needed to maintain high pressure; cook 35 minutes. Remove from heat; let stand 10 minutes or until pressure releases. Remove lid.

3 Stir in hominy; bring to a boil over high heat. Cook 10 minutes or until slightly thick, stirring occasionally. Stir in cilantro.

SERVES 7 (SERVING SIZE: ABOUT 1½ CUPS)
CALORIES 281; **FAT** 9G (SAT 2G, MONO 4.1G, POLY 1.8G); **PROTEIN** 21G;
CARB 28G; **FIBER** 5G; **CHOL** 50MG; **IRON** 2MG; **SODIUM** 750MG; **CALC** 37MG

15 MINUTE PREP!

Chipotle-Apricot
PULLED PORK BBQ

This sweet and slightly spicy pork sandwich would pair well with a crisp slaw on the side.

PREP: 15 MINUTES   **UNDER PRESSURE:** 45 MINUTES   **TOTAL:** 1 HOUR 15 MINUTES

1½ cups diced onion
1⅓ cups water
½ cup cider vinegar
4 pounds boneless pork shoulder (Boston butt), trimmed and cut into 4 pieces
1 to 2 chipotle chiles, canned in adobo sauce

½ cup apricot fruit spread
½ cup barbecue sauce
1 tablespoon grated orange rind
¼ teaspoon salt
8 (1.8-ounce) whole-wheat hamburger buns, toasted

1 Combine first 4 ingredients (through pork) in a 6-quart pressure cooker. Chop chiles, and add to cooker. Close lid securely; bring to high pressure over high heat (about 9 minutes). Reduce heat to medium or level needed to maintain high pressure; cook 45 minutes. Remove from heat; let stand 6 minutes or until pressure releases. Remove lid.

2 Remove pork from cooker with a slotted spoon. Shred with 2 forks; keep warm. Skim fat from surface of cooking liquid; discard. Bring cooking liquid to a simmer over low heat. Stir in fruit spread and next 3 ingredients (through salt); simmer 2 minutes. Stir in pork and any accumulated juices. Cover and let stand 5 minutes. Serve pork mixture on buns.

SERVES 8 (SERVING SIZE: ABOUT ½ CUP PORK MIXTURE AND 1 BUN)
CALORIES 380; **FAT** 10G (SAT 3.1G, MONO 4G, POLY 2G); **PROTEIN** 29G;
CARB 44G; **FIBER** 4.7G; **CHOL** 17MG; **IRON** 3MG; **SODIUM** 523MG; **CALC** 82MG

PAELLA with Cilantro

Make sure you buy Spanish chorizo, which is already cooked. You can find it in the meat section at most grocery stores.

PREP: 15 MINUTES **UNDER PRESSURE:** 16 MINUTES **TOTAL:** 51 MINUTES

1 tablespoon canola oil
1½ cups uncooked short-grain brown rice
1½ cups chopped onion
2 bay leaves
2¼ cups water, divided
1 cup dry white wine
1 cup grape tomatoes, halved
1½ teaspoons smoked paprika
1 teaspoon ground cumin
1 pound mussels, scrubbed and debearded
1 pound large shrimp, peeled and deveined
6 ounces Spanish chorizo, diced
½ cup frozen green peas, thawed
½ cup chopped fresh cilantro
¾ teaspoon salt
8 lemon wedges

1 Heat a 6-quart pressure cooker over medium-high heat. Add oil to cooker; swirl to coat. Add rice, onion, and bay leaves; cook 2 minutes, stirring frequently. Stir in 2 cups water and wine.

2 Close lid securely; bring to high pressure over high heat (about 4 minutes). Adjust heat to medium or level to maintain high pressure; cook 16 minutes. Remove from heat; let stand 6 minutes or until pressure releases. Remove lid.

3 Stir in ¼ cup water, tomatoes, and next 5 ingredients (through chorizo). Cover (do not lock), and cook over medium heat 5 minutes or until mussels open and shrimp are done, stirring occasionally. Discard any unopened shells. Remove from heat; stir in peas, cilantro, and salt. Remove and discard bay leaves. Let stand 3 minutes. Serve with lemon wedges.

SERVES 8 (SERVING SIZE: 1 CUP PAELLA AND 1 LEMON WEDGE)
CALORIES 330; **FAT** 8G (SAT 2.1G, MONO 1.5G, POLY 1.1G); **PROTEIN** 23G; **CARB** 36G; **FIBER** 3G; **CHOL** 100MG; **IRON** 4MG; **SODIUM** 880MG; **CALC** 80MG

PRESSURE PERFECT TIP:
Discard any mussels that don't open during cooking.

JAMBALAYA

Andouille, a spiced, heavily smoked sausage, is the signature ingredient in this classic Creole dish.

PREP: 15 MINUTES   UNDER PRESSURE: 16 MINUTES   TOTAL: 60 MINUTES

1 teaspoon canola oil
1½ cups (⅛-inch-thick) slices andouille sausage (8 ounces)
1 pound bone-in chicken breast halves, skinned
2½ cups water
1¼ cups uncooked long-grain brown rice
1 cup chopped onion
1 cup chopped red bell pepper
1 cup chopped green bell pepper
1 cup sliced celery
1 teaspoon dried thyme
¼ teaspoon ground red pepper
3 bay leaves
2 teaspoons Old Bay seasoning
1 pound jumbo shrimp, peeled and deveined
1 (14.5-ounce) can diced tomatoes with green pepper, celery, and onion, drained
Sliced green onions (optional)

1 Heat a 6-quart pressure cooker over medium-high heat. Add oil to cooker; swirl to coat. Add sausage; cook 4 minutes or until browned, stirring frequently. Remove sausage from cooker. Add chicken to drippings in cooker; cook 2 minutes on each side or until lightly browned.

2 Stir in 2½ cups water and next 8 ingredients (through bay leaves). Close lid securely; bring to high pressure over high heat (about 6 minutes). Adjust heat to medium or level to maintain high pressure; cook 16 minutes. Remove from heat; place cooker under cold running water. Remove lid.

3 Stir in sausage, Old Bay seasoning, shrimp, and tomatoes. Bring to a boil over high heat. Reduce heat to medium, and cook 5 minutes or until shrimp are done, stirring frequently. Remove from heat; let stand 15 minutes before serving. Garnish with sliced green onions, if desired.

SERVES 8 (SERVING SIZE: ABOUT 1 CUP)
CALORIES 310; FAT 9G (SAT 2.5G, MONO 0.9G, POLY 0.6G); PROTEIN 27G; CARB 25G; FIBER 2G; CHOL 130MG; IRON 1G; SODIUM 850MG; CALC 60MG

SWAP IN A SNAP: Use smoked ham or chorizo if you can't find andouille.

Spicy Asian
CHICKEN THIGHS

Serve these saucy chicken thighs over cooked noodles
with a side of steamed broccoli for a well-rounded meal.

PREP: 15 MINUTES   **UNDER PRESSURE:** 15 MINUTES   **TOTAL:** 53 MINUTES

8 bone-in chicken thighs
   (about 1¾ pounds), skinned
1 cup water
½ cup hoisin sauce
¼ cup rice vinegar
1 tablespoon brown sugar
2 tablespoons minced peeled
   fresh ginger
1 tablespoon minced fresh
   garlic
2 tablespoons sambal oelek
   (ground fresh chile paste)
2 tablespoons fresh lime juice
1 tablespoon dark sesame oil
Cooking spray
¼ cup thinly sliced green
   onions
¼ cup cilantro leaves
Lime wedges (optional)

1 Pat chicken dry with a paper towel. Combine 1 cup water and next 8 ingredients (through sesame oil) in a large bowl. Add chicken, turning to coat. Place chicken mixture in a 6-quart pressure cooker. Close lid securely; bring to high pressure over medium-high heat (about 6 minutes). Adjust heat to medium or level to maintain high pressure; cook 15 minutes. Remove from heat; place cooker under cold running water. Remove lid.

2 While chicken mixture cooks, preheat broiler.

3 Line a jelly-roll pan with foil; coat foil with cooking spray. Remove chicken from cooker with tongs, and place on prepared pan. Broil chicken 3 minutes on each side or until crisp and lightly charred.

4 While chicken broils, bring cooking liquid to a simmer over high heat; cook 5 minutes or until slightly thick.

5 Sprinkle chicken with green onions and cilantro; serve with sauce and, if desired, lime wedges.

SERVES 8 (SERVING SIZE: 1 CHICKEN THIGH AND ¼ CUP SAUCE)
CALORIES 180; **FAT** 8G (SAT 2G, MONO 2.9G, POLY 2.7G); **PROTEIN** 15G;
CARB 10G; **FIBER** 1G; **CHOL** 50MG; **IRON** 1MG; **SODIUM** 510MG; **CALC** 15MG

PRESSURE PERFECT TIP:
Finish these chicken thighs in the broiler to ensure a crispy outside and a juicy inside.

Middle Eastern-Spiced
CHICKEN AND TOMATOES

Thighs can withstand longer cooking times and still remain juicy,
which makes them excellent for the pressure cooker.

PREP: 10 MINUTES   **UNDER PRESSURE:** 19 MINUTES   **TOTAL:** 1 HOUR 10 MINUTES

1 tablespoon olive oil
6 skinless, boneless chicken thighs (about 2 pounds)
1 cup diced onion
½ cup slivered almonds
1½ cups water
½ cup pimiento-stuffed olives
1½ teaspoons ground cumin
¼ teaspoon ground red pepper
1 (14.5-ounce) can stewed tomatoes, undrained
1 cup uncooked whole-wheat Israeli couscous
½ cup raisins
½ cup chopped fresh cilantro
½ teaspoon salt

1 Heat a 6-quart pressure cooker over medium-high heat. Add oil to cooker; swirl to coat. Add chicken; cook 6 minutes, turning to brown all sides. Remove chicken from cooker. Add onion and almonds to cooker; cook 2 minutes or until lightly browned, stirring frequently. Return chicken and any accumulated juices to cooker. Stir in 1½ cups water, olives, and next 3 ingredients (through tomatoes).

2 Close lid securely; bring to high pressure over high heat (about 6 minutes). Adjust heat to medium or level to maintain high pressure; cook 15 minutes. Remove from heat; place cooker under cold running water. Remove lid.

3 Remove chicken from cooker. Add couscous and raisins to tomato mixture in cooker. Close lid securely; bring to high pressure over high heat (about 5 minutes). Adjust heat to medium or level to maintain high pressure; cook 4 minutes. Remove from heat; place cooker under cold running water. Remove lid.

4 Gently stir in cilantro and salt; top with chicken. Partially cover, and let stand 5 minutes before serving.

SERVES 6 (SERVING SIZE: ABOUT ⅔ CUP COUSCOUS MIXTURE AND 1 CHICKEN THIGH)
CALORIES 490; **FAT** 18.7G (SAT 3.5G, MONO 9.8G, POLY 4.1G); **PROTEIN** 37G; **CARB** 45G; **FIBER** 6G; **CHOL** 155MG; **IRON** 3MG; **SODIUM** 690MG; **CALC** 73MG

**SWAP
IN A SNAP:**
Kalamata olives make a good substitute for the pimiento-stuffed variety—just be sure they have no pits.

Tomatillo-Braised
CHICKEN THIGHS

The tomatillos in this sauce offer a tangy contrast to the rich chicken flavor.

PREP: 10 MINUTES   **UNDER PRESSURE:** 6 MINUTES   **TOTAL:** 30 MINUTES

12 ounces tomatillos (about 4 medium), husks removed
1 medium jalapeño pepper, halved and seeded
1 cup chopped fresh cilantro
½ cup unsalted chicken stock
1½ teaspoons all-purpose flour
6 garlic cloves
8 bone-in chicken thighs (about 1¾ pounds), skinned
½ teaspoon salt
½ teaspoon freshly ground black pepper
2 cups hot cooked white rice
3 tablespoons Mexican crema
Additional chopped fresh cilantro (optional)
Red jalapeño slices (optional)
Lime wedges (optional)

1 Preheat broiler.

2 Arrange tomatillos and jalapeño pepper halves on a jelly-roll pan. Broil 9 minutes, turning after 5 minutes. Let cool slightly. Peel tomatillos and jalapeño pepper halves. Place tomatillos, jalapeño pepper halves, cilantro, and next 3 ingredients (through garlic) in a blender; process until smooth.

3 Sprinkle chicken with salt and pepper. Add chicken to a 6-quart pressure cooker; pour tomatillo mixture over chicken. Close lid securely; bring to high pressure over high heat (about 4 minutes). Adjust heat to medium or level to maintain high pressure; cook 6 minutes. Remove from heat; place cooker under cold running water. Remove lid. Remove chicken from cooker; keep warm. Bring tomatillo mixture to a boil over medium-high heat; cook 3 to 4 minutes or until slightly thick. Serve chicken and tomatillo sauce over rice; top with Mexican crema. Garnish with additional chopped fresh cilantro, jalapeño slices, and lime wedges, if desired.

SERVES 4 (SERVING SIZE: ½ CUP RICE, 2 CHICKEN THIGHS, ABOUT ¼ CUP TOMATILLO SAUCE, AND ABOUT 2 TABLESPOONS MEXICAN CREMA)
CALORIES 380; **FAT** 14G (SAT 4.5G, MONO 4.0G, POLY 2.7G); **PROTEIN** 32G; **CARB** 30G; **FIBER** 2G; **CHOL** 110MG; **IRON** 3MG; **SODIUM** 390MG; **CALC** 45MG

CHICKEN CACCIATORE

This brightly flavored chicken and vegetable combination would be excellent served over pasta or rice. Leftovers will be welcome, as the sauce will develop more flavor overnight.

PREP: 20 MINUTES   **UNDER PRESSURE:** 9 MINUTES   **TOTAL:** 51 MINUTES

1 tablespoon olive oil
1¼ cups chopped onion
¾ cup chopped red bell pepper
½ cup thinly sliced celery
2 large garlic cloves, finely minced
4 ounces presliced mushrooms
½ cup dry white wine
2 teaspoons chopped fresh thyme
1½ teaspoons chopped fresh oregano
½ teaspoon salt
¼ teaspoon crushed red pepper
¼ teaspoon freshly ground black pepper
2 bay leaves
1 (3½-pound) whole chicken, skinned and cut into pieces
1 (14-ounce) can whole tomatoes, undrained and chopped
2 tablespoons chopped fresh parsley
1½ teaspoons grated lemon rind

1 Heat a 6-quart pressure cooker over medium-high heat. Add oil to cooker; swirl to coat. Add onion and next 3 ingredients (through garlic); sauté 3 minutes. Add mushrooms; sauté 3 minutes. Stir in wine and next 6 ingredients (through bay leaves). Add chicken pieces, and top with tomatoes (do not stir).

2 Close lid securely; bring to high pressure over high heat (about 9 minutes). Adjust heat to medium or level to maintain high pressure; cook 9 minutes. Remove from heat; place cooker under cold running water. Remove lid. Remove bay leaves; discard.

3 Transfer chicken pieces to a serving platter. Bring vegetable mixture to a boil; reduce heat to medium-low, and simmer 10 minutes or until slightly thick, stirring occasionally. Spoon vegetable mixture over chicken; sprinkle with parsley and lemon rind.

SERVES 4 (SERVING SIZE: ¼ OF CHICKEN AND ¾ CUP VEGETABLE MIXTURE)
CALORIES 530; **FAT** 14G (SAT 3G, MONO 5.6G, POLY 3.1G); **PROTEIN** 76G;
CARB 15G; **FIBER** 5G; **CHOL** 240MG; **IRON** 4MG; **SODIUM** 800MG; **CALC** 85MG

SWAP IN A SNAP:
1 teaspoon dried thyme and ¾ teaspoon dried oregano can be substituted for fresh.

BRAISED CHICKEN
with Honey-Lemon Leeks

Lemon is a bright partner for the caramelized leeks and melds beautifully with the honey.

PREP: 20 MINUTES   **UNDER PRESSURE:** 9 MINUTES   **TOTAL:** 51 MINUTES

4 teaspoons olive oil, divided
8 bone-in, skinless chicken
   thighs (about 2 pounds)
3/4 teaspoon kosher salt,
   divided
1/2 teaspoon freshly ground
   black pepper
1 tablespoon grated lemon rind
4 cups thinly sliced leek (about
   3 large)
3 tablespoons fresh lemon
   juice
2 teaspoons honey
2 tablespoons chopped fresh
   parsley or chives (optional)
Lemon wedges (optional)

1 Heat a 6-quart pressure cooker over medium heat. Add 2 teaspoons oil to cooker; swirl to coat. Sprinkle chicken evenly with 1/2 teaspoon salt and pepper. Massage lemon rind into chicken. Add chicken to cooker. Close lid securely; bring to high pressure over high heat (about 9 minutes). Adjust heat to medium or level to maintain high pressure; cook 9 minutes. Remove from heat; place cooker under cold running water. Remove lid. Remove chicken from cooker, and place on a platter; keep warm.

2 Add 2 teaspoons oil to cooker; swirl to coat. Add leek and 1/4 teaspoon salt; cook 15 minutes or until leek begins to brown, scraping pan to loosen browned bits. Remove pan from heat; stir in lemon juice and honey. Top chicken with leek mixture. If desired, sprinkle with fresh parsley or chives and serve with lemon wedges.

SERVES 4 (SERVING SIZE: 2 THIGHS AND ABOUT 1/4 CUP LEEK MIXTURE)
CALORIES 339; **FAT** 15.6G (SAT 3.6G, MONO 7.7G, POLY 2.8G); **PROTEIN** 33G;
CARB 17G; **FIBER** 5G; **CHOL** 0MG; **IRON** 4MG; **SODIUM** 492MG; **CALC** 72MG

PRESSURE PERFECT TIP:
Select chicken thighs that are equal in size so they will cook evenly.

QUICKER POULTRY!

Cooking versatile chicken and turkey in your pressure cooker is super easy and can save time when compared to other traditional oven or stovetop methods. Here are some speedier ways to cook your favorite cuts of poultry.

START HERE!

1. Sprinkle chicken with salt, pepper, and desired seasonings. Assemble the cuts or brown the cuts on each side according to the chart. Add 2 cups of desired liquid.

2. Close lid securely; bring to high pressure over high heat (about 5 minutes) and maintain pressure according to chart.

3. Remove from heat; place cooker under cold running water. Remove lid. If needed, simmer chicken on stovetop until liquid is thickened to desired consistency.

WHOLE CHICKEN
TOTAL TIME: 37 MINUTES

Place 1 (6-pound) whole chicken in a 6-quart pressure cooker. Add liquid, and cook under pressure 22 minutes.

BONELESS CHICKEN BREASTS
TOTAL TIME: 22 MINUTES

Heat a 6-quart pressure cooker over medium-high heat. Add 1 tablespoon oil to cooker; swirl to coat. Add 4 (6-ounce) boneless chicken breasts; cook 6 minutes, turning to brown all sides. Add liquid, and cook under pressure 7 minutes.

BONE-IN CHICKEN BREAST
TOTAL TIME: 23 MINUTES
Heat a 6-quart pressure cooker over medium-high heat. Add 1 tablespoon oil to cooker; swirl to coat. Add 4 (8-ounce) bone-in breasts; cook 6 minutes, turning to brown all sides. Add liquid, and cook under pressure 8 minutes.

BONELESS CHICKEN THIGHS
TOTAL TIME: 22 MINUTES
Heat a 6-quart pressure cooker over medium-high heat. Add 1 tablespoon oil to cooker; swirl to coat. Add 4 (8-ounce) boneless thighs; cook 6 minutes, turning to brown all sides. Add liquid, and cook under pressure 7 minutes.

BONE-IN CHICKEN THIGHS
TOTAL TIME: 20 MINUTES
Heat a 6-quart pressure cooker over medium-high heat. Add 1 tablespoon oil to cooker; swirl to coat. Add 8 (5 to 7-ounce) bone-in thighs; cook 6 minutes, turning to brown all sides. Add liquid, and cook under pressure 5 minutes.

BONE-IN TURKEY BREAST
TOTAL TIME: 53 MINUTES
Place 1 (6-pound) bone-in turkey breast in a 6-quart pressure cooker. Add liquid, and cook under pressure 35 minutes.

CHICKEN FRICASSEE

PREP: 25 MINUTES   **UNDER PRESSURE:** 6 MINUTES   **TOTAL:** 60 MINUTES

4.5 ounces all-purpose flour
(about 1 cup)

4 chicken leg quarters (about
2¹⁄₂ pounds), skinned

¹⁄₂ teaspoon kosher salt

¹⁄₂ teaspoon freshly ground
black pepper

1 tablespoon butter

1 tablespoon olive oil

1 pound cremini mushrooms,
quartered

³⁄₄ cup dry white wine

3 thyme sprigs

2 sage sprigs

1¹⁄₄ cups fat-free, lower-sodium
chicken broth

1 pound baby carrots

10 ounces pearl onions, peeled

1 tablespoon chopped fresh
thyme

1 tablespoon chopped
fresh sage

1 Weigh or lightly spoon flour into a dry measuring cup; level with a knife. Place flour in a shallow dish. Sprinkle chicken with salt and pepper. Dredge chicken in flour. Melt butter in an 8-quart pressure cooker over medium-high heat. Add oil to cooker; swirl to coat. Place 2 chicken leg quarters, flesh sides down, in cooker; cook 5 minutes or until browned. Remove from pan; set aside, and keep warm. Repeat procedure with 2 chicken leg quarters.

2 Add mushrooms to cooker; sauté 5 minutes or until liquid evaporates. Remove mushrooms from cooker using a slotted spoon; set aside, and keep warm.

3 Add wine to cooker, scraping pan to loosen browned bits. Bring to a boil; cook 30 seconds. Tie twine around thyme and sage sprigs. Add chicken, herb sprigs, and broth to cooker. Close lid securely; bring to high pressure over high heat (about 4 minutes). Reduce heat to medium or level needed to maintain high pressure; cook 6 minutes. Remove from heat; place cooker under cold running water. Remove lid.

4 Add mushrooms, carrots, and onions to cooker. Close lid securely; return cooker to high pressure over high heat (about 8 minutes). Immediately remove from heat; place cooker under cold running water. Remove lid. Remove chicken and vegetables from cooker with a slotted spoon. Arrange chicken and vegetables on a platter; keep warm.

5 Bring cooking liquid to a boil over medium-high heat; reduce heat, and simmer until reduced to 1 cup (about 12 minutes). Remove herb sprigs; discard. Add chopped thyme and chopped sage to cooking liquid. Serve chicken and vegetables with cooking liquid.

SERVES 4 (SERVING SIZE: 1 CHICKEN LEG QUARTER, ABOUT 1¹⁄₃ CUPS VEGETABLES, AND ABOUT ¹⁄₄ CUP COOKING LIQUID)
CALORIES 398; **FAT** 12G (SAT 3.7G, MONO 4.9G, POLY 2.1G); **PROTEIN** 34G; **CARB** 38G; **FIBER** 6G; **CHOL** 112MG; **IRON** 4MG; **SODIUM** 659MG; **CALC** 108MG

Beer-Braised Chicken Sandwiches
WITH CABBAGE SLAW

The sweet-and-sour slaw would also be great as a side with grilled chicken or chicken sausage.

PREP: 12 MINUTES **UNDER PRESSURE:** 8 MINUTES **TOTAL:** 25 MINUTES

4 bone-in chicken thighs (about 1¾ pounds), skinned
½ teaspoon kosher salt
½ teaspoon freshly ground black pepper
1 cup brown ale
1 teaspoon all-purpose flour
¼ teaspoon sugar
4 teaspoons grainy mustard, divided
2 tablespoons cider vinegar
1 tablespoon olive oil
2 cups finely shredded red cabbage
1 cup julienne-cut Granny Smith apple
1 tablespoon chopped dill pickle
4 (1-ounce) slices rye bread (about ½ inch thick)

1 Heat a 6-quart pressure cooker over medium-high heat. Sprinkle chicken with salt and pepper. Place chicken in cooker. Combine beer, flour, and sugar in a medium bowl, stirring with a whisk until smooth. Pour beer mixture over chicken in cooker.

2 Close lid securely; bring to high pressure over high heat (about 4 minutes). Adjust heat to medium or level to maintain high pressure; cook 8 minutes. Remove from heat; place cooker under cold running water. Remove lid.

3 Remove chicken from cooker; let stand 5 minutes. Remove chicken from bones; shred. Discard bones. Bring cooking liquid to a boil, scraping cooker to loosen browned bits; cook until reduced to ½ cup (about 4 minutes). Stir in 1 tablespoon mustard. Return shredded chicken to cooker; toss gently to coat.

4 Combine vinegar, oil, and 1 teaspoon mustard in a bowl, stirring with a whisk. Add cabbage, apple, and pickle; toss to coat.

5 Place about ½ cup chicken mixture on each bread slice; top with about ¾ cup cabbage mixture.

SERVES 4 (SERVING SIZE: 1 OPEN-FACED SANDWICH)
CALORIES 390; **FAT** 16.1G (SAT 3.5G, MONO 7G, POLY 3.8G); **PROTEIN** 31G;
CARB 24G; **FIBER** 3G; **CHOL** 100MG; **IRON** 3MG; **SODIUM** 570MG; **CALC** 49MG

SWAP IN A SNAP: A lager-style beer would also work in this recipe.

CHICKEN
with Carrots and Potatoes

All you need is 10 minutes to get this dish in the pressure cooker. If you don't care to use the wine, you can use ½ cup of additional chicken broth.

PREP: 10 MINUTES   **UNDER PRESSURE:** 8 MINUTES   **TOTAL:** 25 MINUTES

1¾ cups vertically sliced onion
Cooking spray
2 cups baby carrots
6 small round red potatoes (about 1 pound), cut into ¼-inch slices
½ cup fat-free, lower-sodium chicken broth
½ cup dry white wine
1 tablespoon chopped fresh thyme
1 teaspoon minced fresh garlic
¾ teaspoon salt, divided
½ teaspoon freshly ground black pepper, divided
1 teaspoon paprika
6 (6-ounce) bone-in chicken thighs, skinned
1 teaspoon olive oil
Chopped fresh thyme (optional)

1 Place onion in a 6-quart pressure cooker coated with cooking spray; top with carrots and potatoes.

2 Combine broth, next 3 ingredients (through garlic), ½ teaspoon salt, and ¼ teaspoon pepper. Pour over vegetables.

3 Combine paprika, ¼ teaspoon salt, and ¼ teaspoon pepper; rub over chicken. Heat a large nonstick skillet over medium-high heat. Add oil to pan; swirl to coat. Add chicken. Cook 3 minutes on each side or until browned. Arrange chicken on top of vegetables.

4 Close lid securely; bring to high pressure over high heat (about 4 minutes). Adjust heat to medium or level to maintain high pressure; cook 8 minutes. Remove from heat; place cooker under cold running water. Remove lid.

5 Remove from cooker. Garnish with additional thyme, if desired.

SERVES 6 (SERVING SIZE: 1 CHICKEN THIGH AND 1½ CUPS VEGETABLE MIXTURE)
CALORIES 300; **FAT** 10G (SAT 2.5G, MONO 4.1G, POLY 2.3G); **PROTEIN** 26G; **CARB** 20G; **FIBER** 3G; **CHOL** 85MG; **IRON** 2MG; **SODIUM** 440MG; **CALC** 38MG

BRAISED CHICKEN
with Kale

Vinegar, stirred in at the end, gives a hit of acid and balances the bitterness of the kale.

PREP: 10 MINUTES   **UNDER PRESSURE:** 8 MINUTES   **TOTAL:** 26 MINUTES

- 4 chicken leg quarters (about 2½ pounds), skinned
- ½ teaspoon freshly ground black pepper
- ¼ teaspoon salt
- 1.1 ounces all-purpose flour (about ¼ cup)
- 2 tablespoons canola oil, divided
- 5 garlic cloves, chopped
- 1 (16-ounce) package cut pre-washed kale (such as Glory Foods)
- 1 (14.5-ounce) can unsalted fire-roasted diced tomatoes, drained
- 1 (14.5-ounce) can fat-free, lower-sodium chicken broth
- 1 tablespoon red wine vinegar

1 Sprinkle chicken with pepper and salt. Weigh or lightly spoon flour into a dry measuring cup; level with a knife. Place flour in a shallow dish; dredge chicken in flour. Heat a 6-quart pressure cooker over medium-high heat. Add 2 teaspoons oil to cooker; swirl to coat. Place half of chicken in cooker; cook 1½ minutes on each side. Remove from cooker. Repeat procedure with 2 teaspoons oil and remaining chicken.

2 Add 2 teaspoons oil to cooker. Add garlic; sauté 20 seconds. Gradually add kale, stirring until kale wilts. Stir in tomatoes and broth. Return chicken to pan. Close lid securely; bring to high pressure over high heat (about 3 minutes). Adjust heat to medium or level to maintain high pressure; cook 8 minutes. Remove from heat; place cooker under cold running water. Remove lid.

3 Remove chicken from pan. Stir vinegar into kale mixture. Serve chicken over kale mixture.

SERVES 4 (SERVING SIZE: 1 CHICKEN LEG QUARTER AND 1½ CUPS KALE MIXTURE)
CALORIES 470; **FAT** 22G (SAT 4.5G, MONO 9.7G, POLY 5.6G); **PROTEIN** 46G; **CARB** 22G; **FIBER** 5G; **CHOL** 135MG; **IRON** 5MG; **SODIUM** 760MG; **CALC** 209MG

PRESSURE PERFECT TIP: Coating the chicken in flour before searing helps to thicken the sauce.

CHICKEN AND SWEET POTATOES
with Raspberry-Balsamic Reduction

Perfect for any weeknight, these succulent chicken pieces take about 30 minutes to prepare. The sweet and sticky sauce makes this dish taste like you spent all day making it.

PREP: 15 MINUTES   **UNDER PRESSURE:** 7 MINUTES   **TOTAL:** 32 MINUTES

- 2 tablespoons lower-sodium soy sauce
- 2 tablespoons balsamic vinegar
- 2 teaspoons Worcestershire sauce
- ¼ teaspoon salt
- ¼ teaspoon crushed red pepper
- 1 tablespoon canola oil
- 4 chicken drumsticks (about 1 pound), skinned
- 4 chicken thighs (about 1 pound), skinned
- 5 shallots, peeled (about 7 ounces)
- ½ cup water
- ¼ teaspoon freshly ground black pepper
- 2 large peeled sweet potatoes (about 1 pound), cut into 2-inch pieces
- ½ cup raspberry spreadable fruit (such as Smucker's Simply Fruit)

1 Combine first 5 ingredients in a medium bowl; set aside.

2 Heat a 6-quart pressure cooker over medium-high heat. Add 1½ teaspoons oil to cooker; swirl to coat. Add half of chicken to cooker; cook 4 minutes, browning on all sides. Remove chicken from cooker, and keep warm. Repeat procedure with 1½ teaspoons oil and remaining half of chicken. Add shallots to cooker; cook 2 minutes, stirring frequently. Add ½ cup water, scraping cooker to loosen browned bits; stir in black pepper. Place chicken on top of shallots; top with sweet potato, and drizzle with 2 tablespoons soy sauce mixture. Do not stir.

3 Close lid securely; bring to high pressure over high heat (about 7 minutes). Adjust heat to medium or level to maintain high pressure; cook 7 minutes. Remove from heat; place cooker under cold running water. Remove lid.

4 Remove chicken, potato, and shallots with a slotted spoon, and place on a platter. Add remaining soy sauce mixture and spreadable fruit to cooking liquid in cooker. Bring to a boil over high heat; cook until reduced to 1 cup (about 2 minutes), stirring constantly. Spoon sauce over chicken, potatoes, and shallots.

SERVES 4 (SERVING SIZE: 1 CHICKEN DRUMSTICK, 1 CHICKEN THIGH, ¾ CUP SWEET POTATO MIXTURE, AND ABOUT ¼ CUP SAUCE)
CALORIES 530; **FAT** 13G (SAT 2.5G, MONO 5.6G, POLY 3.2G); **PROTEIN** 47G; **CARB** 52G; **FIBER** 5G; **CHOL** 210MG; **IRON** 3MG; **SODIUM** 750MG; **CALC** 72MG

POTATO, CORN, and CHICKEN STEW (AJIACO)

PREP: 15 MINUTES UNDER PRESSURE: 20 MINUTES TOTAL: 42 MINUTES

15 MINUTE PREP!

1 tablespoon olive oil, divided
12 chicken thighs (about 4 pounds), skinned
3½ cups fat-free, lower-sodium chicken broth, divided
1½ cups fresh corn kernels (about 3 ears), divided
½ cup chopped onion
½ cup thinly sliced carrot
1½ cups water
1½ teaspoons chopped fresh oregano
1 teaspoon chopped fresh thyme
2½ cups finely shredded peeled baking potato
2½ cups cubed peeled Yukon gold or red potato
¼ cup chopped fresh cilantro
1 tablespoon fresh lime juice
¼ teaspoon salt
½ teaspoon hot pepper sauce (such as Tabasco)
¼ teaspoon freshly ground black pepper
¾ cup cubed peeled avocado
4½ teaspoons capers

1 Heat a 6-quart pressure cooker over medium-high heat. Add 1½ teaspoons oil to cooker; swirl to coat. Add half of chicken; cook 5 minutes, browning on all sides. Remove chicken from cooker. Repeat procedure with remaining half of chicken. Remove from cooker; discard drippings.

2 Place 1 cup broth and ½ cup corn in a food processor; process until corn is pureed.

3 Return cooker to medium-high heat. Add 1½ teaspoons oil to cooker; swirl to coat. Add onion and carrot; sauté 2 minutes. Stir in pureed corn mixture, 2½ cups broth, 1 cup corn, 1½ cups water, oregano, and thyme. Stir in baking potato. Return chicken thighs to cooker. Close lid securely; bring to high pressure over high heat (about 16 minutes). Adjust heat to medium to maintain high pressure; cook 20 minutes. Remove from heat; place cooker under cold running water. Remove lid. Remove chicken from cooker; cool slightly.

4 Remove chicken from bones, discarding bones. Shred chicken into bite-sized pieces. Return shredded chicken to cooker. Stir in cilantro and next 4 ingredients (through black pepper); cook, uncovered, 5 minutes, stirring frequently. Ladle stew into bowls; top with avocado and capers.

SERVES 9 (SERVING SIZE: 1½ CUPS STEW, 4 TEASPOONS AVOCADO, AND ½ TEASPOON CAPERS)
CALORIES 319; FAT 15.4G (SAT 3.8G, MONO 6.9G, POLY 3.2G); PROTEIN 31G; CARB 14G; FIBER 2.3G; CHOL 102MG; IRON 2MG; SODIUM 535MG; CALC 24MG

6 STEPS
to Perfectly Cooked
CHICKEN

Making a whole chicken in a pressure cooker
is a handy technique because it's almost hands free.
Season the chicken and vegetables—then let the
pressure cooker do the rest of the work.

1. CHOOSE A SMALL CHICKEN

You want to be sure you select a chicken that fits
in a 6-quart pressure cooker. Purchase one that's
6 pounds or smaller.

2. SEASON THE VEGGIES AND BIRD

Coat the vegetables and chicken well with
seasonings so they'll absorb during cooking.
Place the veggies in the pot first.

3. TOP THE VEGGIES WITH THE BIRD

Place the chicken on top of the vegetables. This will allow the juices from the chicken to absorb into the vegetables.

4. REMOVE THE CHICKEN

Carefully remove the chicken with 2 large spoons; place the chicken on a platter.

5. SAVE THE DRIPPINGS

Use a slotted spoon to remove the vegetables, leaving the drippings behind to make a sauce or gravy.

6. MAKE A SAUCE

Skim the fat from the surface of the cooking liquid; discard. Stir in flour, and cook to brown; add broth, wine, or a mixture of both for your base sauce.

CHICKEN
with Rich Lemon-Herb Sauce

The secret's definitely in the sauce...so is the flavor. Don't skip the last step—it brings it all together.

PREP: 15 MINUTES **UNDER PRESSURE:** 22 MINUTES **TOTAL:** 57 MINUTES

2 teaspoons chopped fresh thyme

2 teaspoons paprika

1 teaspoon chopped fresh dill

1 teaspoon salt

½ teaspoon freshly ground black pepper

1 pound red potatoes (about 12), cut into 1-inch pieces

8 ounces green beans, trimmed and cut into 2-inch pieces

1 small onion, cut into 8 wedges

2 tablespoons minced fresh garlic, divided

1 tablespoon olive oil

1 (3½-pound) roasting chicken, skinned

1 cup water

3 tablespoons fresh lemon juice

1 tablespoon all-purpose flour

1 tablespoon cold water

1 Combine first 5 ingredients in a small bowl. Combine potato, green beans, onion, and 1 tablespoon garlic in a large bowl; drizzle with oil, and sprinkle with 2½ teaspoons spice mixture, tossing to coat.

2 Remove and discard giblets and neck from chicken. Trim excess fat. Sprinkle chicken with remaining spice mixture; rub with 1 tablespoon garlic.

3 Pour 1 cup water into a 6-quart pressure cooker. Add potato mixture; place chicken on top of potato mixture. Drizzle lemon juice over chicken.

4 Close lid securely; bring to high pressure over high heat (about 7 minutes). Adjust heat to medium or level to maintain high pressure; cook 22 minutes. Remove from heat; let stand 8 minutes or until pressure releases. Remove lid.

5 Carefully remove chicken with 2 large spoons; place chicken on a platter. Remove vegetables with a slotted spoon, and place around chicken on platter. Skim fat from surface of cooking liquid; discard. Combine flour and 1 tablespoon cold water, stirring with a whisk. Bring cooking liquid to a boil over medium-high heat. Add flour mixture, stirring with a whisk. Return to a boil; reduce heat, and simmer 5 minutes or until slightly thick. Serve chicken and vegetables with sauce.

SERVES 4 (SERVING SIZE: ¼ OF CHICKEN, ABOUT 1 CUP VEGETABLES, AND ABOUT 3 TABLESPOONS SAUCE)
CALORIES 390; **FAT** 9.8G (SAT 2G, MONO 4.4G, POLY 1.7G); **PROTEIN** 44G; **CARB** 27G; **FIBER** 4G; **CHOL** 130MG; **IRON** 3MG; **SODIUM** 750MG; **CALC** 64MG

COCONUT-RED CURRY
Hot Pot with Braised Chicken and Mushrooms

Look for Kaffir lime leaves and galangal—also known
as Thai ginger—at ethnic markets and gourmet grocers.

PREP: 20 MINUTES UNDER PRESSURE: 8 MINUTES TOTAL: 60 MINUTES

2 cups fat-free, lower-sodium
  chicken broth
³/₄ cup chopped peeled fresh
  lemongrass
6 Kaffir lime leaves, torn
5 (¹/₄-inch) slices fresh galangal
1¹/₂ tablespoons red curry paste
8 ounces skinless, boneless
  chicken breast, cut into
  bite-sized pieces
6 tablespoons coarsely chopped
  fresh cilantro, divided
2 tablespoons fresh lime juice
1 tablespoon Thai fish sauce
2 teaspoons brown sugar
1 (13.66-ounce) can light
  coconut milk
1 (4-ounce) package presliced
  exotic mushroom blend
  (such as shiitake, cremini,
  and oyster)
3 ounces uncooked wide rice
  noodles
¹/₃ cup thinly sliced green
  onions

1 Bring broth to a boil in a 6-quart pressure cooker over medium-high heat; stir in lemongrass, lime leaves, and galangal. Reduce heat, and simmer 5 minutes. Remove from heat; let stand 30 minutes. Strain broth mixture through a sieve into a bowl; discard solids.

2 Return broth to cooker; add curry paste, stirring with a whisk. Add chicken, ¼ cup cilantro, lime juice, and next 4 ingredients (through mushroom blend). Close lid securely; bring to high pressure over high heat (about 4 minutes). Adjust heat to medium or level to maintain high pressure; cook 8 minutes. Remove from heat; place cooker under cold running water. Remove lid.

3 While chicken mixture cooks, cook rice noodles according to package directions; drain. Add cooked noodles and green onions to chicken mixture. Divide chicken mixture among 6 bowls; sprinkle with remaining cilantro.

SERVES 6 (SERVING SIZE: ABOUT 1 CUP)
CALORIES 150; **FAT** 3.5G (SAT 2G, MONO 0.3G, POLY 0.2G); **PROTEIN** 10G; **CARB** 19G; **FIBER** 1G; **CHOL** 30MG; **IRON** 1MG; **SODIUM** 510MG; **CALC** 22MG

SWAP IN A SNAP:
If you can't find Kaffir lime leaves, use an extra ¼ cup chopped and peeled lemongrass.

Mexican
CHICKEN STEW

Ground guajillo chile powder found in Mexican markets is quite different from regular chili powder.

PREP: 5 MINUTES   **UNDER PRESSURE:** 20 MINUTES   **TOTAL:** 47 MINUTES

3 pounds chicken pieces, skinned

2 cups thinly sliced onion

¾ teaspoon salt

½ teaspoon coarsely ground black pepper

3 (14.5-ounce) cans fat-free, lower-sodium chicken broth

4 garlic cloves, crushed

3 bell peppers, seeded and chopped

1 bay leaf

1 (15-ounce) can golden or white hominy, drained

2 tablespoons ground guajillo chile powder

1½ teaspoons dried oregano

½ cup roasted unsalted pumpkinseed kernels

¼ cup chopped fresh cilantro

¼ cup sliced radishes

¼ cup sliced green onions

½ cup crumbled queso fresco cheese

1 Combine chicken and next 7 ingredients (through bay leaf) in a 6-quart pressure cooker. Close lid securely; bring to high pressure over high heat (about 16 minutes). Adjust heat to medium or level needed to maintain high pressure; cook 20 minutes. Remove from heat; place cooker under cold running water. Remove lid. Remove chicken from broth mixture; cool slightly. Remove chicken from bones; cut chicken into bite-sized pieces. Discard bones.

2 Strain stock through a sieve over a bowl; discard solids. Return stock to cooker; stir in chicken, hominy, chile powder, and oregano. Let stand 5 minutes. Skim fat from surface of broth; discard.

3 Ladle stew into 8 bowls; top each serving evenly with pumpkinseed kernels, cilantro, radishes, green onions, and queso fresco cheese.

SERVES 8 (SERVING SIZE: ABOUT 1 CUP STEW)
CALORIES 213; **FAT** 6.7G (SAT 2.3G, MONO 1.9G, POLY 1.6G); **PROTEIN** 25G; **CARB** 14G; **FIBER** 3G; **CHOL** 56MG; **IRON** 2MG; **SODIUM** 483MG; **CALC** 88MG

Rustic Chicken Soup
WITH NOODLES

PREP: 20 MINUTES   UNDER PRESSURE: 20 MINUTES   TOTAL: 1 HOUR 12 MINUTES

1 tablespoon canola oil
1½ cups chopped onion
4 carrots, peeled and cut
    into 1-inch pieces
3 celery stalks, cut into
    1-inch pieces
1½ teaspoons chopped
    peeled fresh ginger
½ teaspoon salt
½ teaspoon freshly ground
    black pepper

7 garlic cloves, peeled
2 bay leaves
1 (3½-pound) whole chicken,
    skinned
3 cups fat-free, lower-
    sodium chicken broth
2 cups water, divided
3 ounces uncooked wide egg
    noodles
¼ cup chopped fresh
    parsley

1 Heat a 6-quart pressure cooker over medium-high heat. Add oil to cooker; swirl to coat. Add onion, carrot, and celery; sauté 5 minutes or just until tender. Stir in ginger and next 4 ingredients (through bay leaves); cook 1 minute. Place chicken, breast side up, in cooker; cover with broth and 1 cup water.

2 Close lid securely; bring to high pressure over medium-high heat (about 10 minutes). Adjust heat to low or level to maintain high pressure; cook 20 minutes. Remove from heat; place cooker in a large bowl or roasting pan. Release pressure using pressure release valve. Remove lid. Transfer chicken to a cutting board; cool 10 minutes. Shred meat, discarding bones and any remaining skin. Bring cooking liquid to a boil over medium-high heat. Stir in noodles; cook 6 minutes or until tender. Stir in shredded chicken, 1 cup water, and parsley.

SERVES 8 (SERVING SIZE: 1 CUP)
CALORIES 200; **FAT** 5G (SAT 0.9G, MONO 2.1G, POLY 1.4G); **PROTEIN** 23G;
CARB 15G; **FIBER** 2G; **CHOL** 75MG; **IRON** 2MG; **SODIUM** 430MG; **CALC** 44MG

CHICKEN-BARLEY SOUP

Using chicken stock guarantees more flavor than traditional broth and a nicer golden color in the soup.

PREP: 10 MINUTES **UNDER PRESSURE:** 17 MINUTES **TOTAL:** 48 MINUTES

3 cups unsalted chicken stock
2 cups water
2 cups diced carrot
1 cup diced peeled Yukon Gold or red potato
1 cup diced onion
3/4 cup sliced celery
1/2 cup uncooked pearl barley
1 tablespoon chopped fresh oregano
1/2 teaspoon salt
1/2 teaspoon freshly ground black pepper
1 bay leaf
2 cups shredded skinless, boneless rotisserie chicken breast
Additional chopped fresh oregano (optional)
Additional freshly ground black pepper (optional)

1 Combine first 11 ingredients (through bay leaf) in a 6-quart pressure cooker. Close lid securely; bring to high pressure over high heat (about 6 minutes). Adjust heat to medium or level to maintain high pressure; cook 17 minutes. Remove from heat; let stand 12 minutes or until pressure releases. Remove lid.

2 Add chicken to cooker. Cook over medium heat 3 minutes or until thoroughly heated. Sprinkle with additional oregano and pepper, if desired.

SERVES 6 (SERVING SIZE: ABOUT 2 CUPS)
CALORIES 180; **FAT** 2G (SAT 0G, MONO 0.6G, POLY 0.2G); **PROTEIN** 16G; **CARB** 24G; **FIBER** 4G; **CHOL** 40MG; **IRON** 1MG; **SODIUM** 420MG; **CALC** 40MG

CHICKEN, SHRIMP, and VEGETABLE GUMBO

This hearty dish freezes well and tastes even better the next day. Serve in bowls as is or over rice.

PREP: 20 MINUTES   **UNDER PRESSURE:** 20 MINUTES   **TOTAL:** 65 MINUTES

1.1 ounces all-purpose flour (about ¼ cup)
¼ cup canola oil
1½ cups diced green bell pepper
1 cup diced onion
1 cup chopped celery
1 garlic clove, chopped
3 cups water
1 tablespoon Old Bay seasoning
1 teaspoon garlic powder
½ teaspoon salt
2 (14.5-ounce) cans stewed tomatoes, undrained
1½ pounds skinless, boneless chicken thighs, cut into 1-inch pieces
4 bay leaves
1 tablespoon hot sauce
1 pound peeled and deveined medium shrimp
1 pound okra, cut into 1-inch pieces

1 Heat a 6-quart pressure cooker over medium-high heat. Weigh or lightly spoon flour into a dry measuring cup; level with a knife. Combine flour and oil in cooker; cook 5 minutes, stirring constantly with a flat spatula until dark brown.

2 Reduce heat to medium. Add bell pepper and next 3 ingredients (through garlic); cook 3 minutes, stirring often. Stir in 3 cups water and next 6 ingredients (through bay leaves).

3 Close lid securely; bring to high pressure over high heat (about 6 minutes). Adjust heat to medium or level to maintain high pressure; cook 20 minutes. Remove from heat; let stand 16 minutes or until pressure releases. Remove lid.

4 Stir in hot sauce, shrimp, and okra. Cook over medium heat 5 minutes or until okra is tender and shrimp are done, stirring occasionally. Remove and discard bay leaves.

SERVES 8 (SERVING SIZE: 1½ CUPS)
CALORIES 280; **FAT** 11G (SAT 1.5G, MONO 5.8G, POLY 3G); **PROTEIN** 27G; **CARB** 16G; **FIBER** 3G; **CHOL** 150MG; **IRON** 17G; **SODIUM** 109MG; **CALC** 111MG

PRESSURE PERFECT TIP:
Cook the shrimp and okra without pressure for the best texture.

"ROAST" TURKEY
with Thyme Gravy

No need to heat up the kitchen with the oven
when you can cook a turkey in 40 minutes in one pot!

PREP: 20 MINUTES **UNDER PRESSURE:** 40 MINUTES **TOTAL:** 1 HOUR 15 MINUTES

1½ cups water
1 medium onion, cut into thin
   slices
2 teaspoons smoked paprika
1 teaspoon salt
½ teaspoon onion powder
½ teaspoon ground cumin
1 (6- to 7-pound) bone-in turkey
   breast
2 tablespoons all-purpose flour
3 tablespoons cold water
1 tablespoon thyme leaves
½ teaspoon freshly ground
   black pepper

1 Place 1½ cups water and onion slices in a 9-quart pressure cooker. Combine paprika and next 3 ingredients (through cumin) in a small bowl. Loosen skin from turkey by inserting fingers, gently pushing between skin and meat. Rub half of seasoning mixture under loosened skin; rub remaining seasoning mixture over outside of turkey. Place turkey in cooker.

2 Close lid securely; bring to high pressure over high heat (about 7 minutes). Adjust heat to medium or level to maintain high pressure; cook 40 minutes. Remove from heat; let stand 6 minutes or until pressure releases. Remove lid. Remove turkey from cooker; cut into slices, and keep warm. Discard skin.

3 Strain cooking liquid through a sieve into a 1-quart glass measure, pressing gently on solids to release liquid. Discard fat and solids. Return cooking liquid to cooker.

4 Place flour in a small bowl; gradually add 3 tablespoons cold water, stirring with a whisk. Bring cooking liquid to a boil over medium-high heat. Add flour mixture, stirring with a whisk until smooth. Reduce heat to medium-low; cook 1 minute or until thick, stirring constantly. Stir in thyme and pepper. Serve turkey with gravy.

SERVES 10 (SERVING SIZE: ABOUT 6 OUNCES TURKEY AND ABOUT 2½ TABLESPOONS GRAVY)
CALORIES 260; **FAT** 3.5G (SAT 1G, MONO 1.1G, POLY 1G); **PROTEIN** 55G; **CARB** 2G; **FIBER** 0G; **CHOL** 135MG; **IRON** 2G; **SODIUM** 400MG; **CALC** 18MG

FRESH VEGGIES

BRUSSELS SPROUTS
with Bacon

Brussels sprouts combine with bacon to create one delicious and quick-cooking side dish.

PREP: 10 MINUTES   UNDER PRESSURE: 2 MINUTES   TOTAL: 29 MINUTES

3 center-cut bacon slices, finely chopped
¼ teaspoon dried thyme
1½ cups chopped onion
1 cup fat-free, lower-sodium chicken broth
1 pound Brussels sprouts, trimmed and halved

1 Cook bacon in a 6-quart pressure cooker over medium-high heat (do not close lid). Remove bacon from pan with a slotted spoon; drain. Add thyme and onion to pan; sauté 3 minutes. Add broth and Brussels sprouts.

2 Close lid securely; bring to high pressure over high heat (about 6 minutes). Adjust heat to medium or level needed to maintain high pressure; cook 2 minutes. Remove from heat; let stand 6 minutes. Place cooker under cold running water. Remove lid.

3 Sprinkle with bacon.

SERVES 4 (SERVING SIZE: ABOUT 1 CUP)
CALORIES 81; FAT 1.5G (SAT 0.5G, MONO 0.1G, POLY 0.2G); PROTEIN 6.1G; CARB 14G; FIBER 5G; CHOL 4MG; IRON 2G; SODIUM 101MG; CALC 58MG

SWAP IN A SNAP:
You can use ham or pancetta in place of bacon.

BEETS
with Dill and Walnuts

Beets are ready when they can be pierced with a fork without too much resistance. If they're not quite tender enough, put them back under pressure for a minute or two. Prep the dressing while the beets cook.

PREP: 25 MINUTES **UNDER PRESSURE:** 10 MINUTES **TOTAL:** 45 MINUTES

2 pounds beets (about 6)
2½ cups water
1 tablespoon cider vinegar
1 tablespoon fresh lemon juice
2 teaspoons sugar
1½ teaspoons Dijon mustard
¾ teaspoon kosher salt
½ teaspoon freshly ground black pepper
3 tablespoons extra-virgin olive oil
2 tablespoons chopped fresh dill
2 tablespoons finely chopped walnuts

1 Leave root and 1 inch of stem on beets; scrub with a brush. Place beets in a 6-quart pressure cooker; add 2½ cups water. Close lid securely; bring to high pressure over high heat (about 6 minutes). Adjust heat to medium or level needed to maintain high pressure; cook 10 minutes. Remove from heat; let stand 6 minutes. Place cooker under cold running water. Remove lid. Drain beets, and rinse with cold water. Drain; cool. Trim off beet roots; rub off skins. Cut beets in half vertically; cut each half into 4 wedges. Place beets in a medium bowl.

2 Combine vinegar and next 5 ingredients (through pepper) in a small bowl; stir with a whisk. Slowly add oil, stirring constantly with a whisk until combined. Drizzle oil mixture over beets; toss gently. Let stand 15 minutes, tossing gently every 5 minutes. Stir in dill. Top with walnuts just before serving.

SERVES 6 (SERVING SIZE: ¾ CUP)
CALORIES 148; **FAT** 8.5G (SAT 1.1G, MONO 5.3G, POLY 1.8G); **PROTEIN** 3G; **CARB** 17G; **FIBER** 4G; **CHOL** 0MG; **IRON** 1MG; **SODIUM** 370MG; **CALC** 27MG

SWAP IN A SNAP: You can use basil or oregano in place of the dill.

PEACH SALAD
with Tomatoes and Beets

Golden beets and a mix of colorful tomatoes (like Purple Cherokee and red heirlooms) offer a dramatic contrast on the plate and are a beautiful, tasty base or the tangy-sweet peaches. But red beets and any garden tomatoes would also work.

PREP: 15 MINUTES **UNDER PRESSURE:** 10 MINUTES **TOTAL:** 35 MINUTES

2 medium-sized golden beets
2½ cups water
2 medium-sized ripe tomatoes
¾ teaspoon kosher salt, divided
½ teaspoon freshly ground black pepper
3 tablespoons extra-virgin olive oil
2 tablespoons fresh lemon juice, divided
1 tablespoon honey
1 medium shallot, thinly sliced
3 medium peaches, sliced
3 tablespoons small mint leaves
2 teaspoons thyme leaves
2 ounces goat cheese, crumbled (about ½ cup)

1 Leave root and 1 inch of stem on beets; scrub with a brush. Place beets in a 6-quart pressure cooker; add 2½ cups water. Close lid securely; bring to high pressure over high heat (about 6 minutes). Adjust heat to medium or level needed to maintain high pressure; cook 10 minutes. Remove from heat; let stand 6 minutes. Place cooker under cold running water. Remove lid. Drain beets, and rinse with cold water. Drain; cool. Trim off beet roots; rub off skins. Cut beets into ¼-inch-thick slices. Place beets in a medium bowl.

2 Core tomatoes; cut into ¼-inch-thick slices. Arrange beet and tomato slices on a platter; sprinkle with ½ teaspoon salt and pepper.

3 Combine ¼ teaspoon salt, oil, 1 tablespoon juice, honey, and shallot in a medium bowl. Toss peach slices with 1 tablespoon juice. Add peach mixture to honey mixture; toss. Mound peach mixture on top of beet and tomato slices; sprinkle salad with mint, thyme, and goat cheese.

SERVES 8 (SERVING SIZE: ABOUT 2 BEET SLICES, 2 TOMATO SLICES, AND ½ CUP PEACH MIXTURE)
CALORIES 112; **FAT** 6.8G (SAT 2G, MONO 4.1G, POLY 0.7G); **PROTEIN** 3G; **CARB** 12G; **FIBER** 2G; **CHOL** 3MG; **IRON** 1G; **SODIUM** 164MG; **CALC** 23G

HEIRLOOM TOMATO and BEET SALAD

This salad delivers a vibrant and delicious dish showcasing summer's sweet, juicy tomatoes.

PREP: 15 MINUTES **UNDER PRESSURE:** 10 MINUTES **TOTAL:** 35 MINUTES

- 2 medium-sized red beets
- 2 medium-sized golden beets
- 2½ cups water
- 3 tablespoons chopped fresh chives
- 2 tablespoons chopped fresh tarragon
- 2 tablespoons chopped shallots
- 1 tablespoon capers
- 3 tablespoons extra-virgin olive oil
- 2 tablespoons balsamic vinegar
- 1 teaspoon Dijon mustard
- 3 cups heirloom cherry tomatoes, halved
- 2 pounds heirloom tomatoes, sliced
- ½ teaspoon kosher salt
- ¼ teaspoon freshly ground black pepper

1 Leave root and 1 inch of stem on beets; scrub with a brush. Place beets in a 6-quart pressure cooker; add 2½ cups water. Close lid securely; bring to high pressure over high heat (about 6 minutes). Adjust heat to medium or level needed to maintain high pressure; cook 10 minutes. Remove from heat; let stand 6 minutes. Place cooker under cold running water. Remove lid. Drain beets, and rinse with cold water. Drain; cool. Trim off beet roots; rub off skins. Slice beets.

2 Combine chives and next 6 ingredients (through mustard) in a small bowl, stirring with a whisk. Combine cherry tomatoes and about 5 teaspoons mustard mixture; toss to coat. Divide sliced beets and sliced tomatoes among 6 plates. Drizzle each serving with remaining mustard mixture. Top each serving with cherry tomatoes. Sprinkle with salt and pepper.

SERVES 6 (SERVING SIZE: ABOUT 3 BEET SLICES, ABOUT 4 TOMATO SLICES, ABOUT 3 TEASPOONS DRESSING, AND ½ CUP CHERRY TOMATOES)
CALORIES 137; **FAT** 7.8G (SAT 1G, MONO 5G, POLY 0.9G); **PROTEIN** 3G; **CARB** 15G; **FIBER** 4G; **CHOL** 0MG; **IRON** 1G; **SODIUM** 275MG; **CALC** 35G

PRESSURE PERFECT TIP: Select beets that are equal in size to ensure even cooking.

Cauliflower and Fennel with
DIJON-CIDER VINAIGRETTE

This simple side of cauliflower dressed in a vinaigrette may be just the ticket to get you past your childhood aversion to this veggie. The dijon-cider vinaigrette is what really seals the deal.

PREP: 10 MINUTES   **UNDER PRESSURE:** 2 MINUTES   **TOTAL:** 24 MINUTES

1 large head cauliflower
1 cup water
1 cup sliced fennel
¼ cup olive oil
1 tablespoon chopped fresh fennel fronds
2 tablespoons cider vinegar
2 teaspoons Dijon mustard
1 teaspoon honey
¼ teaspoon kosher salt
¼ teaspoon freshly ground black pepper

1 Place cauliflower in a 6-quart pressure cooker; add 1 cup water. Close lid securely; bring to high pressure over high heat (about 6 minutes). Adjust heat to medium or level needed to maintain high pressure; cook 2 minutes. Remove from heat; let stand 6 minutes. Place cooker under cold running water. Remove lid. Chop cauliflower into florets. Toss with fennel.

2 Combine oil and remaining ingredients in a large bowl, stirring with a whisk. Add cauliflower mixture; toss to coat.

SERVES 6 (SERVING SIZE: ABOUT 1 CUP)
CALORIES 118; **FAT** 9.3G (SAT 1.3G, MONO 6.6G, POLY 1G); **PROTEIN** 2G; **CARB** 8G; **FIBER** 3G; **CHOL** 0MG; **IRON** 1G; **SODIUM** 161MG; **CALC** 32MG

SWAP IN A SNAP:
For variation, try this recipe with broccoli rather than the cauliflower.

CAULIFLOWER SOUP
with Shiitakes

Pureed cauliflower creates a wonderfully creamy soup; meaty shiitakes add textural flair.

PREP: 10 MINUTES   **UNDER PRESSURE:** 3 MINUTES   **TOTAL:** 20 MINUTES

10 MINUTE PREP!

4 teaspoons olive oil, divided
¾ cup thinly sliced leek, white and light green parts only
⅜ teaspoon kosher salt, divided
4 cups coarsely chopped cauliflower florets (about 1 medium head)
1½ cups unsalted chicken stock (such as Swanson), divided
¾ cup water
2 teaspoons chopped fresh thyme
¼ cup 2% reduced-fat milk
1½ teaspoons butter
¼ teaspoon white pepper
1 (3.5-ounce) package shiitake mushroom caps
1 teaspoon lower-sodium Worcestershire sauce
1 teaspoon sherry vinegar
2 teaspoons chopped fresh parsley

1 Heat a 6-quart pressure cooker over medium-high heat. Add 2 teaspoons oil to cooker; swirl to coat. Add leek; sauté 1 minute. Add ⅛ teaspoon salt. Cook 5 minutes or until leeks are softened, stirring occasionally. Add cauliflower, 1 cup and 6 tablespoons stock, ¾ cup water, and thyme. Close lid securely; bring to high pressure over high heat (about 5 minutes). Adjust heat to medium or level to maintain high pressure; cook 3 to 4 minutes. Remove from heat; place cooker under cold running water. Remove lid.

2 Place cauliflower mixture in a blender. Remove center piece of blender lid (to allow steam to escape); secure blender lid on blender. Place a clean towel over opening in blender lid (to avoid splatters). Blend until smooth. Return to saucepan. Stir in ¼ teaspoon salt, milk, butter, and pepper. Keep warm.

3 Thinly slice mushroom caps. Heat a large skillet over medium-high heat. Add 2 teaspoons oil to pan, and swirl to coat. Add mushrooms; sauté 6 minutes or until browned. Add 2 tablespoons stock, Worcestershire sauce, and sherry vinegar. Cook 1 minute or until liquid is reduced and syrupy.

4 Ladle soup into each of 4 bowls. Top each serving with mushroom mixture. Sprinkle evenly with parsley.

SERVES 4 (SERVING SIZE: ABOUT 1 CUP SOUP AND ABOUT 2 TABLESPOONS MUSHROOM MIXTURE)
CALORIES 113; **FAT** 6.7G (SAT 1.8G, MONO 3.8G, POLY 0.6G); **PROTEIN** 5.5G; **CARB** 10.1G; **FIBER** 2.8G; **CHOL** 5MG; **IRON** 1.2MG; **SODIUM** 357MG; **CALC** 63MG

QUICKER VEGGIES!

Cooking dense vegetables like winter squash, cabbage, potatoes, and carrots on the stovetop can take anywhere from 30 minutes to an hour. Here's how to use your pressure cooker to cook them in half the time.

START HERE!

1. Fill a 6-quart pressure cooker with water amount listed in chart; add vegetables.

2. Close lid securely; bring to high pressure over high heat (about 5 to 8 minutes) and maintain pressure according to chart.

3. Remove from heat; place cooker under cold running water. Remove lid. Drain vegetables, and add desired herbs and seasonings.

ARTICHOKES
TOTAL TIME: 20 MINUTES
Add 1 cup water and 4 artichokes (with stems removed, top ¼ removed, and leaves trimmed). Cook under pressure 15 minutes.

BEETS
TOTAL TIME: 25 MINUTES
Add 1 cup water and 1 pound halved (if small) or quartered (if large) beets. Cook under pressure 20 minutes.

BRUSSELS SPROUTS

TOTAL TIME: 7 MINUTES

Add 1 cup water and 1 pound halved Brussels sprouts. Cook under pressure 2 minutes.

BUTTERNUT SQUASH

TOTAL TIME: 17 MINUTES

Add 1 cup water and 1 peeled and seeded butternut squash cut into 1-inch pieces. Cook under pressure 12 minutes.

CABBAGE

TOTAL TIME: 20 MINUTES

Add 1 quart water and 1 head cabbage cut into quarters. Cook under pressure 15 minutes.

RED POTATOES

TOTAL TIME: 12 MINUTES

Add 1½ cups water and 1 pound potatoes cut into ¾-inch-thick pieces. Cook under pressure 7 minutes.

CARROTS

TOTAL TIME: 9 MINUTES

Add 1 cup water and 1 pound peeled carrots cut into ½-inch-thick pieces. Cook under pressure 4 minutes.

15 MINUTE PREP!

Creole
BRAISED CABBAGE

The delicious flavors in this easy cabbage recipe will be perfect with pork or chicken dishes.

PREP: 15 MINUTES   **UNDER PRESSURE:** 10 MINUTES   **TOTAL:** 40 MINUTES

4 center-cut bacon slices
1 medium onion, chopped
4 garlic cloves, minced
1 (2-pound) head green cabbage, halved, cored, and cut into ¼-inch-thick slices (about 12 cups)
⅔ cup fat-free, lower-sodium chicken broth
2 teaspoons chopped fresh oregano
2 teaspoons chopped fresh thyme
½ teaspoon crushed red pepper
¼ teaspoon freshly ground black pepper
1 (14.5-ounce) can diced tomatoes with green pepper, celery, and onion, drained
2 bay leaves
¼ cup chopped fresh parsley

1 Cook bacon in a 6-quart pressure cooker over medium-high heat 7 minutes or until crisp. Remove bacon from cooker, reserving 2 tablespoons drippings in cooker; crumble bacon. Add onion and garlic to drippings in cooker; sauté 4 minutes. Stir in cabbage; cook 2 minutes or until cabbage begins to wilt, stirring frequently. Stir in broth and next 6 ingredients (through bay leaves).

2 Close lid securely; bring to high pressure over medium-high heat (about 6 minutes). Adjust heat to medium or level to maintain high pressure; cook 10 minutes. Remove from heat; place cooker under cold running water. Remove lid.

3 Remove bay leaves; discard. Stir in parsley and crumbled bacon.

SERVES 14 (SERVING SIZE: ½ CUP)
CALORIES 103; **FAT** 6.3G (SAT 1.1G, MONO 4.2G, POLY 1G); **PROTEIN** 2G; **CARB** 5G; **FIBER** 3G; **CHOL** 0MG; **IRON** 1G; **SODIUM** 151MG; **CALC** 32MG

SWAP IN A SNAP:
Canned diced tomatoes seasoned with garlic and onion or basil, garlic, and oregano work well in this recipe.

BRAISED KALE
with Pancetta

Pancetta adds a smoky, bacon-like flavor to the kale.

PREP: 15 MINUTES **UNDER PRESSURE:** 7 MINUTES **TOTAL:** 35 MINUTES

2 pounds kale, chopped
4 cups water
½ teaspoon salt
1 tablespoon canola oil
1 ounce pancetta, finely chopped
½ cup diced onion
1 garlic clove, minced
2 cups unsalted chicken stock
⅛ teaspoon crushed red pepper

1 Combine first 3 ingredients (through salt) in a 6-quart pressure cooker. Close lid securely; bring to high pressure over medium-high heat (about 7 minutes). Adjust heat to medium-low or level to maintain high pressure; cook 7 minutes. Remove from heat; place cooker under cold running water. Remove lid. Drain kale; remove kale from cooker, and keep warm.

2 Heat cooker over medium-high heat. Add oil to cooker; swirl to coat. Add pancetta; cook 3 minutes or until browned. Remove pancetta from cooker. Add onion and garlic to drippings in cooker; sauté 3 minutes or until soft. Add kale, chicken stock, and red pepper; simmer 5 minutes or until kale is tender. Sprinkle with pancetta before serving.

SERVES 4 (SERVING SIZE: 1 CUP)
CALORIES 148; **FAT** 8.5G (SAT 1.1G, MONO 5.3G, POLY 1.8G); **PROTEIN** 3G; **CARB** 17G; **FIBER** 4G; **CHOL** 0MG; **IRON** 1MG; **SODIUM** 370MG; **CALC** 27MG

PRESSURE PERFECT TIP: Be sure to remove the thick stems of the kale.

COLLARD GREENS
with Ham Hocks

You will enjoy old-fashioned Southern flavor in these greens.

PREP: 15 MINUTES   UNDER PRESSURE: 10 MINUTES   TOTAL: 40 MINUTES

1 pound collard greens, stems removed and chopped
6 ounces smoked ham hocks
2 cups water
1/2 teaspoon salt
1/4 teaspoon freshly ground black pepper
1 tablespoon canola oil
1 tablespoon chopped fresh garlic
1 tablespoon brown sugar
1/8 teaspoon crushed red pepper
1 small onion, chopped
1 1/2 cups fat-free, lower-sodium chicken broth
1 tablespoon cider vinegar

1 Combine first 5 ingredients (through black pepper) in a 6-quart pressure cooker. Close lid securely; bring to high pressure over high heat (about 5 minutes). Adjust heat to medium or level to maintain high pressure; cook 10 minutes. Remove from heat; place cooker under cold running water. Remove lid.

2 Drain greens and ham hocks; discard cooking liquid. Remove ham hocks; cool. Remove ham from bones; coarsely chop. Discard bones, skin, and fat.

3 Heat cooker over medium-high heat. Add oil to cooker; swirl to coat. Add garlic and next 3 ingredients (through onion); sauté 5 to 6 minutes or until onion is tender. Stir in greens, ham, broth, and vinegar. Bring to a simmer, and cook 10 minutes or until greens are tender, stirring occasionally.

SERVES 6 (SERVING SIZE: 1/2 CUP)
CALORIES 121; **FAT** 7.4G (SAT 1.1G, MONO 4.2G, POLY 1.6G); **PROTEIN** 2G; **CARB** 15G; **FIBER** 4G; **CHOL** 0MG; **IRON** 1MG; **SODIUM** 360MG; **CALC** 27MG

CURRIED CARROTS
and Parsnips

Fresh cilantro and golden raisins pair nicely
with carrots and parsnips.

PREP: 15 MINUTES   **UNDER PRESSURE:** 4 MINUTES   **TOTAL:** 20 MINUTES

1 tablespoon olive oil
1 pound carrots, peeled and
    cut into 1-inch pieces
1 pound parsnips, peeled and
    cut into 1-inch pieces
2 teaspoons curry powder
1 teaspoon ground cumin
¼ teaspoon ground
    cinnamon

¼ teaspoon salt
⅛ teaspoon ground red
    pepper
1 cup organic vegetable
    broth
½ cup golden raisins
2 tablespoons chopped
    fresh cilantro

1 Heat a 6-quart pressure cooker over medium-high heat. Add oil to cooker; swirl to coat. Add carrots and next 6 ingredients (through red pepper); sauté 1 minute or until spices are lightly toasted. Stir in broth and raisins. Close lid securely; bring to high pressure over high heat (about 3 minutes). Adjust heat to medium or level to maintain high pressure; cook 4 to 6 minutes. Remove from heat; place cooker under cold running water. Remove lid.

2 Remove vegetables from cooker with a slotted spoon, and place on a platter; discard cooking liquid. Sprinkle vegetables with cilantro.

SERVES 8 (SERVING SIZE: ABOUT ½ CUP)
CALORIES 90; **FAT** 3.5G (SAT 1G, MONO 1.3G, POLY 1.1G); **PROTEIN** 1G;
CARB 15G; **FIBER** 4G; **CHOL** 0MG; **IRON** 2G; **SODIUM** 140MG; **CALC** 30MG

Chipotle-Lime
MASHED SWEET POTATOES

The slightly smoky flavor comes from the chipotle chile. Refrigerate the remaining chiles in a resealable plastic bag for another use.

PREP: 15 MINUTES   **UNDER PRESSURE:** 15 MINUTES   **TOTAL:** 30 MINUTES

2 pounds sweet potatoes, peeled and cut into 6 pieces
1 cup water
1/4 teaspoon salt
1 tablespoon brown sugar

2 tablespoons 2% reduced-fat milk
1 tablespoon fresh lime juice
3/4 teaspoon finely chopped chipotle chile, canned in adobo sauce

1 Combine first 3 ingredients (through salt) in a 6-quart pressure cooker. Close lid securely; bring to high pressure over medium-high heat (about 6 minutes). Adjust heat to medium-low or level to maintain high pressure; cook 15 minutes. Remove from heat; place cooker under cold running water. Remove lid.

2 Drain potatoes. Stir in brown sugar and remaining ingredients; mash to desired consistency.

SERVES 6 (SERVING SIZE: 1/2 CUP)
CALORIES 124; **FAT** 7.4G (SAT 1.7G, MONO 4.1G, POLY 1.8G); **PROTEIN** 2G; **CARB** 20G; **FIBER** 2G; **CHOL** 0MG; **IRON** 1MG; **SODIUM** 540MG; **CALC** 27MG

SPICED CARROTS
with Olives and Mint

Transform carrots into an exotic, boldly flavored
Moroccan side dish by braising them with mint, cinnamon,
garlic, red pepper, coriander, honey, and lemon. To finish the dish,
add oil-cured black olives and a splash of oil and vinegar.

PREP: 5 MINUTES   **UNDER PRESSURE:** 5 MINUTES   **TOTAL:** 25 MINUTES

2 cups water
5 cups (1-inch) sliced carrots
   (about 2 pounds)
1½ tablespoons honey
1 tablespoon fresh lemon juice
½ teaspoon sea salt
½ teaspoon coriander seeds
¼ teaspoon crushed red
   pepper
1 (5-inch) mint sprig
1 (2-inch) cinnamon stick
1 garlic clove, minced
¼ cup oil-cured black olives,
   pitted and coarsely chopped
1 teaspoon rice vinegar
1 teaspoon extra-virgin olive oil
1 teaspoon chopped fresh mint
Mint sprigs (optional)

1 Place 2 cups water in a 6-quart pressure cooker. Stir in carrots and next 8 ingredients (through garlic). Close lid securely; bring to high pressure over high heat (about 5 minutes). Adjust heat to medium or level to maintain high pressure; cook 5 minutes. Remove from heat; place cooker under cold running water. Remove lid. Remove carrots with a slotted spoon, reserving liquid.

2 Bring liquid to a boil; cook until reduced to ¼ cup (about 10 minutes). Discard mint sprig and cinnamon stick. Return carrots to pan; stir in olives, vinegar, and oil. Cook 1 minute or until heated. Sprinkle with chopped mint. Garnish with mint sprigs, if desired.

SERVES 5 (SERVING SIZE: ABOUT 1 CUP)
CALORIES 139; **FAT** 4.1G (SAT 0.5G, MONO 2.8G, POLY 0.5G); **PROTEIN** 2.2G;
CARB 25.7G; **FIBER** 5.7G; **CHOL** 0MG; **IRON** 1.1MG; **SODIUM** 470MG; **CALC** 57MG

Sweet Potato
CURRY SOUP

If you prefer your soup with minimal heat,
reduce the curry paste and omit the red chiles.

PREP: 15 MINUTES   **UNDER PRESSURE:** 5 MINUTES   **TOTAL:** 46 MINUTES

1 teaspoon canola oil
1 cup chopped onion
1 garlic clove, chopped
2½ pounds sweet potatoes,
   peeled and cubed
3 cups unsalted chicken stock
1 cup water
3 teaspoons red curry paste
1 teaspoon grated peeled fresh
   ginger
½ teaspoon kosher salt
½ teaspoon ground cumin
1½ tablespoons fresh lime juice
1 (13.66-ounce) can light coconut
   milk
¼ cup cilantro sprigs
2 small Thai red chiles, thinly
   sliced

1 Heat a 6-quart pressure cooker over medium heat. Add oil to cooker; swirl to coat. Add onion; sauté 3 minutes or until soft. Add garlic; sauté 1 minute. Stir in sweet potato and next 6 ingredients (through cumin).

2 Close lid securely; bring to high pressure over high heat (about 8 minutes). Adjust heat to medium or level to maintain high pressure; cook 5 minutes. Remove from heat; place cooker under cold running water. Remove lid. Stir in lime juice and coconut milk. Let stand 15 minutes.

3 Place one-third of potato mixture in a blender. Remove center piece of blender lid (to allow steam to escape); secure blender lid on blender. Place a clean towel over opening in blender lid (to avoid splatters). Blend until smooth. Pour into a large bowl. Repeat procedure twice with remaining potato mixture. Ladle soup into bowls; top evenly with cilantro and chile slices.

SERVES 10 (SERVING SIZE: 1 CUP)
CALORIES 129; **FAT** 7.7G (SAT 2.1G, MONO 3.1G, POLY 1.6G); **PROTEIN** 2G;
CARB 32G; **FIBER** 1G; **CHOL** 0MG; **IRON** 1MG; **SODIUM** 530MG; **CALC** 29MG

PRESSURE PERFECT TIP:
Use small- to medium-sized potatoes—they're sweeter and creamier than the large ones.

6 STEPS
to Perfectly Cooked
POTATOES

The potato is a sturdy vegetable that stands up well to the high heat used during pressure cooking. Try this simple no-fail method for making "twice-baked potatoes."

1. WRAP WITH FOIL

Wrapping the potatoes with foil prevents them from boiling rather than "baking" in the steam.

2. USE WATER

Pour 2½ cups water in the bottom of a 6-quart pressure cooker. The water will create steam to "bake" the potatoes.

3. USE A TRIVET

Place a trivet in the pressure cooker to raise the potatoes off the bottom of the pot. This ensures they'll cook evenly and will prevent them from burning.

4. REMOVE THE POTATOES CAREFULLY

The pot and the potatoes will be very hot. Use tongs to remove the potatoes from the pot.

5. STUFF THEM

Unwrap the potatoes, and cut a 2-inch-wide wedge in the top of each potato. Scoop out the pulp, and combine with the cheese and sour cream. Spoon the mixture back into the potatoes.

6. FINISH IN THE OVEN

Broil in the oven for 2 minutes to melt the cheese and create a crispy exterior.

Rosemary
POTATO WEDGES

Stir the potatoes very frequently while sautéing to prevent sticking.

PREP: 10 MINUTES   **UNDER PRESSURE:** 6 MINUTES   **TOTAL:** 20 MINUTES

- 2 tablespoons olive oil, divided
- 1 pound small red potatoes, quartered
- 1 cup organic vegetable broth
- 2 teaspoons chopped fresh rosemary
- 2 tablespoons grated fresh Parmesan cheese
- ¼ teaspoon kosher salt
- ¼ teaspoon freshly ground black pepper

1 Heat a 6-quart pressure cooker over medium heat. Add 1 tablespoon oil to cooker; swirl to coat. Add potatoes to cooker; sauté 5 minutes or until lightly browned. Add broth to cooker; sprinkle with rosemary.

2 Close lid securely; bring to high pressure over high heat (about 4 minutes). Adjust heat to medium-high or level needed to maintain high pressure; cook 6 minutes. Remove from heat; place cooker under cold running water. Remove lid. Drain potatoes; discard cooking liquid.

3 Place potatoes in a large bowl. Add 1 tablespoon oil, cheese, salt, and pepper; toss gently. Serve immediately.

SERVES 5 (SERVING SIZE: ½ CUP)
CALORIES 110; **FAT** 6.3G (SAT 0.9G, MONO 3.4G, POLY 2.1G); **PROTEIN** 3G;
CARB 25G; **FIBER** 5G; **CHOL** 110MG; **IRON** 3G; **SODIUM** 450MG; **CALC** 120MG

SWAP IN A SNAP: Any herb will work here. Try basil, thyme, or parsley.

Cheddar
MASHED POTATOES

You can also leave the skins on the potatoes for a more rustic version of mashed potatoes.

PREP: 14 MINUTES   **UNDER PRESSURE:** 8 MINUTES   **TOTAL:** 26 MINUTES

2 pounds peeled russet potatoes, cut into ½-inch-thick slices

1 cup water

1 teaspoon salt, divided

1 teaspoon freshly ground black pepper, divided

4 ounces extra-sharp cheddar cheese, shredded (about 1 cup)

¼ cup plus 2 tablespoons 2% reduced-fat milk

½ cup chopped green onions

2 tablespoons reduced-fat sour cream

4 center-cut bacon slices, cooked and crumbled (drained)

1 Place potato, 1 cup water, ½ teaspoon salt, and ½ teaspoon pepper in a 6-quart pressure cooker. Close lid securely; bring to high pressure over medium-high heat (about 6 minutes). Adjust heat to medium-low or level to maintain high pressure; cook 8 minutes. Remove from heat; place cooker under cold running water. Remove lid.

2 Add cheese and milk to potato mixture in cooker; mash to desired consistency. Cook over medium heat 1 minute or until thoroughly heated, stirring constantly. Add ½ teaspoon salt, ½ teaspoon pepper, green onions, sour cream, and bacon, stirring to combine.

SERVES 9 (SERVING SIZE: ½ CUP)
CALORIES 148; **FAT** 8.5G (SAT 1.1G, MONO 5.3G, POLY 1.8G); **PROTEIN** 3G; **CARB** 30G; **FIBER** 4G; **CHOL** 0MG; **IRON** 1MG; **SODIUM** 370MG; **CALC** 27MG

PRESSURE PERFECT TIP:
Adding the salt to the cooking liquid will ensure the potatoes are well seasoned.

STUFFED POTATOES
with Cheese and Sour Cream

Using a pressure cooker is a much quicker alternative to the old-fashioned method of baking the potatoes in the oven before stuffing them—just make sure you use the trivet or rack that comes with your cooker (see page 200).

PREP: 35 MINUTES **UNDER PRESSURE:** 25 MINUTES **TOTAL:** 60 MINUTES

2½ cups water
4 (6-ounce) russet potatoes
3 ounces reduced-fat sharp cheddar cheese, shredded (about ¾ cup)
½ cup reduced-fat sour cream
¼ cup finely chopped green onions, divided
½ teaspoon salt, divided
¼ teaspoon freshly ground black pepper
1 ounce crumbled blue cheese (about ¼ cup)
½ cup grape tomatoes, quartered

1 Pour 2½ cups water into a 6-quart pressure cooker. Place a cooking rack or trivet in bottom of cooker. Wrap potatoes in foil. Arrange potatoes on rack. Close lid securely; bring to high pressure over high heat (about 5 minutes). Adjust heat to medium or level to maintain high pressure; cook 25 minutes. Remove from heat; let stand 9 minutes or until pressure releases. Remove lid.

2 Remove potatoes from cooker with tongs; cool slightly. Unwrap potatoes, and cut a 2-inch wedge out of the top of each potato (do not cut all the way to the bottom of the potato). Scoop out pulp, leaving a ¼-inch-thick shell. Combine potato pulp, cheddar cheese, sour cream, 2 tablespoons green onions, ⅜ teaspoon salt, and pepper in a bowl. Spoon about ⅔ cup potato mixture into each shell; top each with about 1 tablespoon blue cheese and 1½ teaspoons green onions.

3 Preheat broiler. Place stuffed potatoes on a foil-lined baking sheet. Broil 2 minutes or until cheese melts and is lightly browned. Top potatoes with tomatoes, and sprinkle with ⅛ teaspoon salt.

SERVES 4 (SERVING SIZE: 1 STUFFED POTATO)
CALORIES 250; **FAT** 15.6G (SAT 6.5G, MONO 4.2G, POLY 3.1G); **PROTEIN** 15G; **CARB** 45G; **FIBER** 6G; **CHOL** 130MG; **IRON** 25G; **SODIUM** 650MG; **CALC** 105MG

Bacon-Cider
TURNIPS AND APPLES

This sweet and savory side would be a delicious accompaniment to your next holiday dinner.

PREP: 15 MINUTES   **UNDER PRESSURE:** 3 MINUTES   **TOTAL:** 25 MINUTES

4 center-cut bacon slices

2 pounds small turnips, peeled and each cut into 8 wedges (about 6 cups)

1¾ cups vertically sliced onion

2 Fuji apples, peeled and cut into wedges (about 1 pound)

1 cup apple cider

½ teaspoon salt

½ teaspoon freshly ground black pepper

2 tablespoons chopped fresh parsley

1 Cook bacon in a 6-quart pressure cooker over medium heat until crisp. Remove bacon from cooker; crumble. Add turnips, onion, and apple to drippings in cooker; sauté 2 minutes or until lightly browned. Stir in cider, salt, and pepper. Close lid securely; bring to high pressure over high heat (about 5 minutes). Adjust heat to medium or level to maintain high pressure; cook 3 to 4 minutes. Remove from heat; place cooker under cold running water. Remove lid.

2 Place turnip mixture on a serving dish. Sprinkle with crumbled bacon and parsley.

SERVES 8 (SERVING SIZE: ABOUT 1 CUP)
CALORIES 97; **FAT** 2G (SAT 1G, MONO 0.5G, POLY 0.3G); **PROTEIN** 3G; **CARB** 5G; **FIBER** 3G; **CHOL** 50MG; **IRON** 1G; **SODIUM** 340MG; **CALC** 16MG

SWAP IN A SNAP:
Use McIntosh apples instead of the Fuji.

RATATOUILLE-STYLE
Vegetable Sauce

Serve over cooked pasta, baked potatoes, grilled or sautéed chicken breasts, pork chops, fish, or portobello mushroom caps.

PREP: 20 MINUTES **UNDER PRESSURE:** 2 MINUTES **TOTAL:** 60 MINUTES

3 tablespoons extra-virgin olive oil, divided

2 cups diced onion

2 tablespoons chopped fresh basil

¾ teaspoon fennel seeds

¼ teaspoon crushed red pepper

2 (14.5-ounce) cans stewed tomatoes, undrained

2 large red bell peppers, cut into 1-inch pieces

1 pound mushrooms, quartered

1 medium zucchini, halved lengthwise and cut into ½-inch-thick slices

4 cups coarsely chopped fresh spinach

¾ cup coarsely chopped pitted kalamata olives

2 tablespoons tomato paste

1 tablespoon cider vinegar

½ teaspoon salt

1 Heat a 6-quart pressure cooker over medium-high heat. Add 1 tablespoon oil to cooker; swirl to coat. Add onion to cooker; sauté 4 minutes or until lightly browned. Stir in basil and next 6 ingredients (through zucchini).

2 Close lid securely; bring to high pressure over high heat (about 1 minute). Adjust heat to medium or level to maintain high pressure; cook 2 minutes. Remove from heat; place cooker under cold running water. Remove lid.

3 Mash vegetable mixture with a potato masher until slightly thick. Stir in 2 tablespoons oil, spinach, and remaining ingredients. Let stand 30 minutes before serving.

SERVES 9 (SERVING SIZE: 1 CUP)
CALORIES 110; **FAT** 0G (SAT 0G, MONO 0G, POLY 0G); **PROTEIN** 1G; **CARB** 90G; **FIBER** 1G; **CHOL** 0MG; **IRON** 1G; **SODIUM** 457MG; **CALC** 26MG

PRESSURE PERFECT TIP:
Mash the tomatoes after cooking to provide a thick consistency.

Fresh Garlic
MARINARA SAUCE

This zesty sauce is perfect ladled on top of pasta, spooned over chicken, or as a sauce for hot sandwiches.

PREP: 18 MINUTES   **UNDER PRESSURE:** 5 MINUTES   **TOTAL:** 48 MINUTES

¼ cup extra-virgin olive oil, divided

3 cups diced onion

⅓ cup minced fresh garlic

1½ tablespoons sugar

1 tablespoon dried oregano leaves, crumbled

2½ teaspoons salt

¼ teaspoon freshly ground black pepper

¼ teaspoon crushed red pepper

6 (14.5-ounce) cans unsalted diced tomatoes

2 bay leaves

¼ cup tomato paste

¾ cup chopped fresh basil

1 Heat a 6-quart pressure cooker over medium-high heat. Add 1 tablespoon oil to cooker; swirl to coat. Add onion to cooker; sauté 6 minutes or until lightly browned. Add garlic; sauté 30 seconds. Stir in sugar and next 6 ingredients (through bay leaves). Close lid securely; bring to high pressure over medium-high heat (about 29 minutes). Adjust heat to medium or level needed to maintain high pressure; cook 5 minutes. Remove from heat; place cooker under cold running water. Remove lid.

2 Stir in tomato paste; simmer, uncovered, 9 minutes or until slightly thick. Remove from heat. Stir in basil and 3 tablespoons oil.

SERVES 18 (SERVING SIZE: ABOUT ⅔ CUP)
CALORIES 60; **FAT** 0G (SAT 0G, MONO 0G, POLY 0G); **PROTEIN** 1G; **CARB** 4G; **FIBER** 1G; **CHOL** 0MG; **IRON** 1G; **SODIUM** 450MG; **CALC** 20MG

PRESSURE PERFECT TIP:
Allow the sauce to simmer on the stovetop without pressure so it can thicken.

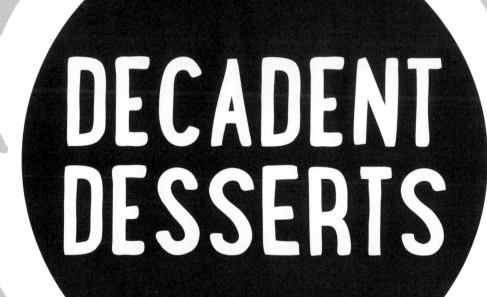

DECADENT DESSERTS

Pomegranate-Poached
PEARS

The natural tartness of pomegranate juice brightens up the pears, while the sweet sour cream mixture adds richness.

PREP: 14 MINUTES **UNDER PRESSURE:** 2 MINUTES **TOTAL:** 26 MINUTES

14 MINUTE PREP!

6 firm ripe medium pears with stems
1½ tablespoons fresh lemon juice
1¾ cups pomegranate juice
⅓ cup dried tart cherries
6 tablespoons granulated sugar
1 teaspoon vanilla extract
2 (3-inch) cinnamon sticks, broken in half
2 whole cloves
¾ cup light sour cream
4 teaspoons brown sugar

1 Peel pears, leaving stems intact. Scoop bottom of core from each pear using the large end of a melon baller. With the small end, scoop out the seeds. If necessary, cut about ¼ inch from base of pears so they will sit flat. Squeeze lemon juice over pears.

2 Combine pomegranate juice and next 5 ingredients (through cloves) in a 6-quart pressure cooker. Place pears, stem ends up, in cooker.

3 Close lid securely, bring to high pressure over high heat (about 5 minutes). Adjust heat to medium or level to maintain high pressure; cook 2 minutes. Remove from heat; place cooker under cold running water. Remove lid.

4 Remove pears with a slotted spoon, and place on a rimmed serving platter. Bring cooking liquid to a boil over high heat; cook until reduced to 1 cup (about 10 minutes). Remove cinnamon sticks and cloves; discard.

5 While cooking liquid boils, combine sour cream and brown sugar in a small bowl, stirring until brown sugar dissolves. Spoon pomegranate sauce over pears, and serve with sour cream mixture.

SERVES 6 (SERVING SIZE: 1 PEAR, ABOUT 3 TABLESPOONS POMEGRANATE SAUCE, AND 2 TABLESPOONS SOUR CREAM MIXTURE)
CALORIES 260; **FAT** 2.5G (SAT 1.5G, MONO 0.1G, POLY 0.1G); **PROTEIN** 2G; **CARB** 62G; **FIBER** 6G; **CHOL** 10MG; **IRON** 1MG; **SODIUM** 40MG; **CALC** 68MG

Fig and Cheese
BRUSCHETTA

Serve leftover compote as a topping for ice cream or as an accompaniment to grilled chicken, beef, or poultry.

PREP: 10 MINUTES   **UNDER PRESSURE:** 5 MINUTES   **TOTAL:** 25 MINUTES

1 cup chopped Granny Smith apple
¾ cup tawny port or other sweet red wine
¾ cup water
½ cup golden raisins
1 (8-ounce) package dried figs, stemmed and quartered
1 (8.5-ounce) whole-wheat French bread baguette, cut into 8 (½-inch-thick) slices
3 ounces Brie cheese, cut into 8 slices
Chopped fresh thyme (optional)

1 Combine first 5 ingredients (through figs) in a 6-quart pressure cooker. Close lid securely; bring to high pressure over high heat (about 4 minutes). Adjust heat to medium or level to maintain high pressure; cook 5 minutes. Remove from heat; let stand 8 minutes or until pressure releases. Remove lid. Let cool.

2 Preheat broiler.

3 Place bread slices on a baking sheet. Broil 1 minute on each side or until lightly toasted. Top each bread slice with 1 cheese slice. Broil 2 to 3 minutes or until cheese melts slightly. Top each with 1 tablespoon fig mixture, and serve immediately. Garnish with thyme, if desired. Cover and chill remaining fig mixture.

SERVES 8 (SERVING SIZE: 1 BRUSCHETTA)
CALORIES 260; **FAT** 4G (SAT 2G, MONO 1.3G, POLY 0.6G); **PROTEIN** 7G; **CARB** 44G; **FIBER** 5G; **CHOL** 10MG; **IRON** 2MG; **SODIUM** 190MG; **CALC** 108MG

SWAP IN A SNAP:
Any dense dried fruit will work in the recipe. Try dried apricots in place of the figs.

RICE PUDDING
with Pears and Raisins

This method of pressure-cooking rice pudding yields a rich, creamy result. It's delicious served warm or chilled.

PREP: 10 MINUTES   **UNDER PRESSURE:** 3 MINUTES   **TOTAL:** 20 MINUTES

3½ cups chopped peeled Bosc pear (about 4 pears)
½ cup raisins
¼ cup apple juice
6 tablespoons sugar, divided
2 (3-inch) cinnamon sticks, divided
4 cups 2% reduced-fat milk
1 cup uncooked Arborio rice or other short-grain rice
3 tablespoons nonfat dry milk
¼ teaspoon ground nutmeg
⅛ teaspoon salt
1 (3-inch) piece vanilla bean, split lengthwise
½ cup heavy cream

1 Combine first 3 ingredients (through apple juice) in a small saucepan. Stir in 3 tablespoons sugar and 1 cinnamon stick; bring to a boil. Reduce heat to low; simmer 10 minutes or until pear is tender, stirring occasionally. Remove cinnamon stick; discard.

2 Combine milk and next 4 ingredients (through salt) in a 6-quart pressure cooker. Stir in 3 tablespoons sugar and 1 cinnamon stick. Scrape seeds from vanilla bean; add seeds and bean to rice mixture. Close lid securely; bring to high pressure over high heat (about 9 minutes). Adjust heat to medium or level to maintain high pressure; cook 3 minutes. Remove from heat; let stand 7 minutes. Place cooker under cold running water. Remove lid. Remove and discard cinnamon stick and vanilla bean. Stir in cream.

3 Divide pear mixture among 8 (8-ounce) ramekins; top with rice mixture. Serve warm, or cover and chill.

SERVES 8 (SERVING SIZE: ABOUT ⅓ CUP PEAR MIXTURE AND ½ CUP RICE MIXTURE)
CALORIES 280; **FAT** 8G (SAT 5G, MONO 2.3G, POLY 0.3G); **PROTEIN** 7G;
CARB 45G; **FIBER** 3G; **CHOL** 30MG; **IRON** 0.5MG; **SODIUM** 110MG; **CALC** 190MG

PRESSURE PERFECT TIP:
Choose a short-grain rice—its high starch content gives this recipe a creamy texture.

RUSTIC APPLESAUCE

This not-too-sweet sauce is perfect eaten alone or served over ice cream as a dessert.

PREP: 6 MINUTES   UNDER PRESSURE: 9 MINUTES   TOTAL: 15 MINUTES

3 pounds Fuji apples, peeled and cut into 1-inch chunks (about 7 cups)
1 cup apple juice
¼ teaspoon ground cinnamon
½ teaspoon vanilla extract
⅛ teaspoon ground allspice
¼ teaspoon salt
2 tablespoons fresh lemon juice
⅓ cup packed brown sugar

1 Combine all ingredients, in the order listed, in a 6-quart pressure cooker. Do not stir. Close lid securely; bring to high pressure over high heat (about 6 minutes). Adjust heat to medium or level to maintain high pressure; cook 9 minutes. Remove from heat; place cooker under cold running water. Remove lid. Stir to break up apples, mashing slightly, if necessary. Serve warm or cold.

SERVES 8 (SERVING SIZE: ½ CUP)
CALORIES 144; **FAT** 0G (SAT 0G, MONO 0G, POLY 0G); **PROTEIN** 0G;
CARB 36G; **FIBER** 4G; **CHOL** 0MG; **IRON** 0MG; **SODIUM** 75MG; **CALC** 18MG

Spicy Pineapple-Mango CHUTNEY

Use this chutney as a topping for grilled pound cake or as a dipping sauce for coconut shrimp.

PREP: 10 MINUTES **UNDER PRESSURE:** 7 MINUTES **TOTAL:** 37 MINUTES

1 tablespoon canola oil
1 tablespoon grated peeled fresh ginger
¼ teaspoon ground cardamom
2½ cups diced peeled mango (about 1 pound)
2 cups chopped pineapple
1¼ cups cider vinegar
1 cup packed brown sugar
½ cup golden raisins
¼ teaspoon salt
1 (3-inch) cinnamon stick
1 tablespoon honey

1 Heat a 6-quart pressure cooker over medium heat. Add oil to cooker; swirl to coat. Add ginger and cardamom; cook 1 minute, stirring constantly.

2 Add mango and next 6 ingredients (through cinnamon stick); stir well. Close lid securely; bring to high pressure over high heat (about 4 minutes). Adjust heat to medium or level to maintain high pressure; cook 7 minutes. Remove from heat; let stand 9 minutes or until pressure releases. Remove lid.

3 Bring mango mixture to a boil over medium heat. Stir in honey. Reduce heat, and simmer 15 minutes or until thick, stirring frequently. Remove from heat; cool. Remove cinnamon stick; discard. Cover and chill.

SERVES 14 (SERVING SIZE: ¼ CUP)
CALORIES 130; **FAT** 1G (SAT 0G, MONO 0.7G, POLY 0.3G); **PROTEIN** 1G; **CARB** 29G; **FIBER** 1G; **CHOL** 0MG; **IRON** 1MG; **SODIUM** 50MG; **CALC** 24MG

Lemon-Lavender
BUNDT CAKE

PREP: 15 MINUTES   **UNDER PRESSURE:** 28 MINUTES   **TOTAL:** 1 HOUR 14 MINUTES

CAKE:

2½ cups water
6.75 ounces all-purpose flour
   (about 1½ cups)
1½ teaspoons dried lavender
½ teaspoon baking powder
½ teaspoon baking soda
¼ teaspoon salt
1 cup granulated sugar
6 tablespoons unsalted butter,
   softened
2 tablespoons canola oil
1 teaspoon grated lemon rind
2 large eggs
½ cup light sour cream
Cooking spray

GLAZE:

1 cup powdered sugar
1 tablespoon fresh lemon juice
1 tablespoon 1% low-fat milk
Fresh or dried lavender flowers
   (optional)

1 To prepare cake, pour 2½ cups water into a 6-quart pressure cooker; place a trivet in bottom of cooker.

2 Weigh or lightly spoon flour into dry measuring cups; level with a knife. Combine flour and next 4 ingredients (through salt) in a medium bowl, stirring with a whisk. Combine granulated sugar, butter, and oil in a large bowl; beat with a mixer at medium speed until light and fluffy. Beat in lemon rind. Add eggs, 1 at a time, beating well after each addition. Add flour mixture and sour cream alternately to sugar mixture, beginning and ending with flour mixture. Spoon batter into a 6-cup Bundt pan coated with cooking spray. Cover with foil, making sure the foil fits tightly around sides and under bottom of pan but leaving room for cake to puff during cooking.

3 Make a sling by folding a sheet of foil in half lengthwise, creating a 6 x 17–inch foil strip. Center pan on foil strip, and lower it carefully into cooker. Fold ends of strip over top of pan. Close lid securely; bring to high pressure over high heat (about 10 minutes). Adjust heat to medium or level to maintain high pressure; cook 28 minutes. Remove from heat; let stand 20 minutes or until pressure releases. Remove lid. Carefully remove pan from cooker using foil sling. Remove foil.

4 Cool in pan 10 minutes on a wire rack. Loosen cake from sides of pan using a narrow metal spatula; turn out onto a wire rack. Cool completely. To prepare glaze, combine powdered sugar, lemon juice, and milk in a small bowl, stirring with a whisk. Spoon glaze over cooled cake. Garnish with lavender flowers, if desired.

SERVES 10 (SERVING SIZE: 1 SLICE)
CALORIES 305; **FAT** 11G (SAT 1G, MONO 4G, POLY 1.2G); **PROTEIN** 4G;
CARB 51G; **FIBER** 0G; **CHOL** 60MG; **IRON** 1MG; **SODIUM** 176MG; **CALC** 32MG

6 STEPS
to Perfectly Cooked
CAKES

With the trivet that comes with your pressure cooker and standard baking ingredients, making a cake under pressure couldn't be easier—just follow these simple steps.

1. ADD WATER TO THE COOKER

Start by pouring water into a pressure cooker; place a trivet in the bottom of the cooker above the water so steam can be used to cook the dessert.

2. WRAP THE PAN IN FOIL

Cover the pan with foil, making sure the foil fits tightly around the sides and under the bottom. This will trap steam in the pan, yielding a moist and evenly cooked dessert.

3. MAKE A SLING

Make a sling by folding a sheet of foil in half lengthwise, creating a 6 x 17–inch foil strip.

4. USE SLING TO INSERT PAN INTO COOKER

Center the pan on the foil strip, and lower it carefully into the cooker. Fold the ends of the strip over the top of the pan.

5. USE SLING TO REMOVE PAN FROM COOKER

Using dry towels or oven mitts, unfold the ends of the strips over the top of the pan. Using two hands, gently lift the pan to remove it from the pot.

6. REMOVE THE FOIL FROM THE PAN

The cake will continue to cook as it rests, so remove the foil while it cools so it doesn't overcook.

BANANA-PECAN
Bundt Cake

PREP: 20 MINUTES   UNDER PRESSURE: 26 MINUTES   TOTAL: 1 HOUR 6 MINUTES

CAKE:
2 cups water
6.75 ounces all-purpose flour
   (about 1½ cups)
½ teaspoon baking soda
½ teaspoon baking powder
¼ teaspoon salt
2 large eggs, lightly beaten
1 cup granulated sugar
¾ cup mashed ripe banana
   (about 2 small)
½ cup low-fat buttermilk
6 tablespoons canola oil
1½ teaspoons vanilla extract,
   divided
⅓ cup chopped pecans,
   toasted
Cooking spray

GLAZE:
¾ cup powdered sugar
2 ounces ⅓-less-fat cream
   cheese, softened (about
   ¼ cup)
3 teaspoons 1% low-fat milk
Chopped pecans

1 To prepare cake, pour 2 cups water into a 6-quart pressure cooker; place a trivet in bottom of cooker.

2 Weigh or lightly spoon flour into dry measuring cups; level with a knife. Combine flour and next 3 ingredients (through salt) in a large bowl, stirring with a whisk. Combine eggs and next 4 ingredients (through oil) in a medium bowl; stir in 1 teaspoon vanilla. Add egg mixture to flour mixture, stirring with a whisk until combined. Stir in pecans. Pour batter into a 6-cup Bundt pan coated with cooking spray. Cover with foil, making sure foil fits around sides and under bottom of pan but leaving room for cake to puff during cooking.

3 Make a sling by folding a sheet of foil in half lengthwise, creating a 6 x 17–inch strip. Center the pan on the foil strip, and lower it carefully into the cooker. Fold the ends of the strip over the top of the pan.

4 Close lid securely; bring to high pressure over high heat (about 3 minutes). Adjust heat to medium or level to maintain high pressure; cook 26 minutes. Remove from heat; let stand 7 minutes or until pressure releases. Remove lid. Blot foil with a towel to remove any water that collected on top of pan. Carefully remove pan from cooker using foil sling; place on a wire rack. Remove foil; cool 10 minutes.

5 Carefully loosen cake from sides of pan using a knife or narrow metal spatula. Invert cake onto wire rack; cool completely. To prepare glaze, place powdered sugar, cream cheese, milk, and ½ teaspoon vanilla in a food processor; process until well blended. Immediately spoon glaze over cooled cake. Sprinkle pecans over glaze.

SERVES 10 (SERVING SIZE: 1 SLICE)
CALORIES 315; **FAT** 14G (SAT 2.1G, MONO 7.2G, POLY 3.8G); **PROTEIN** 5G;
CARB 46G; **FIBER** 2G; **CHOL** 44MG; **IRON** 1MG; **SODIUM** 200MG; **CALC** 38MG

CINNAMON-RAISIN
Bread Pudding

PREP: 20 MINUTES   **UNDER PRESSURE:** 25 MINUTES   **TOTAL:** 1 HOUR 6 MINUTES

½ cup sugar, divided
½ teaspoon ground cinnamon, divided
1 ounce chopped walnuts
1 cup 2% reduced-fat milk
4 large eggs, lightly beaten
1 teaspoon baking powder
2 teaspoons vanilla extract
8 ounces multigrain Italian bread, cubed
¾ cup raisins
Cooking spray
3½ cups water

1 Combine 1 tablespoon sugar with ¼ teaspoon cinnamon in small bowl; set aside. Heat a 6-quart pressure cooker over medium-high heat. Add walnuts, and cook 2 minutes or until beginning to lightly brown, stirring frequently. Set aside.

2 Combine milk, eggs, baking powder, vanilla, and remaining sugar and cinnamon in a large bowl; stir with a whisk. Fold bread cubes into egg mixture. Lightly coat a 5-cup soufflé dish (or a 5-cup stainless steel bowl) with cooking spray; pour bread mixture into dish, and sprinkle with walnuts and raisins. Cover with foil. Make sure the foil fits tightly around the sides and goes under the bottom of dish, but leave room for the pudding to puff during cooking.

3 Place a trivet in bottom of cooker. Make a sling by folding a sheet of foil in half lengthwise, creating a 6 x 17-inch strip. Place soufflé dish in center of sheet. Center dish on the foil strip, and lower it carefully into the cooker. Fold the ends of the strip over the top of the pudding. Pour in enough water to reach one-third up the sides of the pudding dish (about 3½ cups).

4 Close lid securely; bring to high pressure over high heat. Reduce heat to medium or level needed to maintain high pressure; cook 25 minutes. Remove from heat, and let stand 7 minutes or until pressure releases naturally. Remove lid. Make sure there is no water on top of the foil. Remove foil. Carefully remove pan from cooker using foil sling. Sprinkle with reserved cinnamon sugar. Let stand 15 minutes to allow pudding to continue cooking while standing.

SERVES 10 (SERVING SIZE: ¹⁄₁₀ OF BREAD PUDDING)
CALORIES 310; **FAT** 8G (SAT 2G, MONO 1.6G, POLY 3.4G); **PROTEIN** 8G;
CARB 54G; **FIBER** 1G; **CHOL** 80MG; **IRON** 1MG; **SODIUM** 168MG; **CALC** 106MG

Date-Walnut
BREAD PUDDING

PREP: 20 MINUTES **UNDER PRESSURE:** 30 MINUTES **TOTAL:** 1 HOUR 20 MINUTES

4 large eggs, lightly beaten

1¼ cups 2% reduced-fat milk

¾ cup granulated sugar, divided

¼ cup packed brown sugar

2 tablespoons orange-flavored liqueur

1 teaspoon vanilla extract

½ teaspoon ground cinnamon

8 ounces French bread, cut into 1-inch cubes

¾ cup chopped pitted Medjool dates

½ cup chopped walnuts, toasted

Cooking spray

8 cups water

3 tablespoons water

¼ cup half-and-half

1 Combine eggs, milk, ¼ cup granulated sugar, brown sugar, and next 3 ingredients (through cinnamon) in a large bowl. Gently fold in bread, dates, and walnuts. Pour mixture into a 1½-quart soufflé dish coated with cooking spray. Cover with foil, making sure foil fits tightly around sides and under bottom of dish but leaving room for pudding to puff during cooking. Place a trivet in bottom of a 6-quart pressure cooker. Make a sling by folding a sheet of foil in half lengthwise, creating a 6 x 17–inch strip. Center the dish on the foil strip, and lower it carefully into the cooker. Fold the ends of the strip over the top of the dish. Add enough water to cooker to cover 1 inch of dish (about 8 cups).

2 Close lid securely; bring to high pressure over high heat (about 9 minutes). Adjust heat to medium or level to maintain high pressure; cook 30 minutes. Remove from heat; let stand 9 minutes or until pressure releases. Remove lid. Blot foil with a towel to remove any water that collected on top of dish. Carefully remove dish from cooker using foil sling. Remove foil, and let stand 15 minutes.

3 While pudding stands, combine ½ cup granulated sugar and 3 tablespoons water in a medium saucepan. Bring to a boil over medium heat (do not stir). Boil 4 minutes or until sugar mixture is amber, swirling pan occasionally. Remove from heat. Gradually add half-and-half, stirring with a whisk until smooth (be careful of hot steam). If necessary, return to low heat to dissolve caramel, stirring until smooth. Serve bread pudding with caramel sauce.

SERVES 8 (SERVING SIZE: ⅛ OF BREAD PUDDING AND 1 TABLESPOON CARAMEL SAUCE)
CALORIES 231; **FAT** 6.8G (SAT 0.9G, MONO 4.9G, POLY 0.7G); **PROTEIN** 12G; **CARB** 30G; **FIBER** 8G; **CHOL** 0MG; **IRON** 6MG; **SODIUM** 310MG; **CALC** 102MG

Chocolate-Espresso
PUDDING CAKE

PREP: 15 MINUTES   **UNDER PRESSURE:** 10 MINUTES   **TOTAL:** 35 MINUTES

15 MINUTE PREP!

2 cups water
Cooking spray
5 tablespoons sugar, divided
4 ounces bittersweet
   chocolate, chopped
2 tablespoons butter
1.5 ounces all-purpose flour
   (about ⅓ cup)
¼ cup unsweetened cocoa
¼ teaspoon salt
2 large eggs, separated
2 tablespoons coffee-flavored
   liqueur
2 teaspoons instant espresso
   granules
2 cups coffee or vanilla bean
   low-fat ice cream

1 Pour 2 cups water into a 6-quart pressure cooker; place a trivet in bottom of cooker. Coat a 6-inch round cake pan with cooking spray; sprinkle with 1 tablespoon sugar, shaking gently to coat bottom and sides of pan. Combine chocolate and butter in a small microwave-safe bowl. Microwave at HIGH 30 to 45 seconds or until melted.

2 Weigh or lightly spoon flour into a dry measuring cup; level with a knife. Combine flour, cocoa, and salt in a small bowl. Beat egg whites with a mixer at high speed until soft peaks form; gradually add 2 tablespoons sugar, beating until stiff peaks form.

3 Combine egg yolks and 2 tablespoons sugar in a large bowl. Beat with a mixer at high speed until thick and pale. Gradually beat in liqueur, espresso granules, and chocolate mixture. Fold beaten egg whites into egg yolk mixture. Gradually sift flour mixture into egg mixture, and fold in gently. Spoon batter into prepared pan, spreading gently (do not deflate batter). Cover with foil, making sure foil fits tightly around sides and under bottom of pan.

4 Make a sling by folding a sheet of foil in half lengthwise, creating a 6 x 17–inch strip. Center the pan on the foil strip, and lower it carefully into the cooker. Fold the ends of the strip over the top of the cake pan. Close lid securely; bring to high pressure over high heat (about 3 minutes). Adjust heat to medium or level to maintain high pressure; cook 10 minutes. Remove from heat; place cooker under cold running water. Remove lid. Remove pan from cooker using foil sling; place on a wire rack. Remove foil; cool 10 minutes. Spoon warm cake into bowls, and serve immediately with ice cream.

SERVES 8 (SERVING SIZE: ⅛ OF CAKE AND ¼ CUP ICE CREAM)
CALORIES 240; **FAT** 11G (SAT 5G, MONO 1.8G, POLY 1.4G); **PROTEIN** 5G;
CARB 33G; **FIBER** 2G; **CHOL** 563MG; **IRON** 1MG; **SODIUM** 113MG; **CALC** 57MG

Vanilla Bean Cheesecakes
WITH PORT-CHERRY SAUCE

PREP: 20 MINUTES   **UNDER PRESSURE:** 9 MINUTES   **TOTAL:** 5 HOURS

CHEESECAKES:

2 cups water

Cooking spray

2 tablespoons sliced almonds, toasted

8 vanilla wafers

1 (3-inch) piece vanilla bean, split lengthwise

⅓ cup sugar

2 tablespoons all-purpose flour

3 tablespoons fat-free cream cheese

1 (8-ounce) block ⅓ less-fat cream cheese, softened

1 large egg

SAUCE:

½ cup frozen pitted dark sweet cherries

2 tablespoons sugar

1 ½ tablespoons ruby port or other sweet red wine

½ teaspoon cornstarch

2 teaspoons water

1 To prepare cheesecakes, pour 2 cups water into a 6-quart pressure cooker; place a trivet in bottom of cooker. Coat 4 (6-ounce) ramekins or custard cups with cooking spray. Place almonds and vanilla wafers in a food processor; process until finely ground. Divide almond mixture among ramekins, shaking gently to cover bottom of each ramekin. Scrape seeds from vanilla bean; discard bean. Place vanilla bean seeds, ⅓ cup sugar, and next 3 ingredients (through ⅓-less-fat cream cheese) in food processor; process 15 seconds or until smooth. Add egg; process 5 seconds or until blended, scraping sides of bowl as needed. Divide cream cheese mixture among ramekins. Cover and wrap each ramekin entirely with foil. Place ramekins on trivet in cooker.

2 Close lid securely; bring to high pressure over high heat (about 3 minutes). Adjust heat to medium or level to maintain high pressure; cook 9 minutes. Remove from heat; let stand 3 minutes or until pressure releases. Remove lid.

3 Cool cheesecakes slightly. Carefully remove ramekins from cooker; place on a wire rack. Let stand 40 minutes. Cover with plastic wrap, and chill at least 4 hours.

4 To prepare sauce, combine cherries, 2 tablespoons sugar, and port in a small saucepan. Bring to a boil over medium heat, stirring frequently; cook 2 to 3 minutes or until cherries thaw and sugar dissolves. Combine cornstarch and 2 teaspoons water in a small bowl, stirring with a whisk; add to cherry mixture. Return to a boil, and cook 1 minute or until slightly thick, stirring frequently. Serve cheesecakes with sauce.

SERVES 4 (SERVING SIZE: 1 CHEESECAKE AND ABOUT 2 TABLESPOONS SAUCE)
CALORIES 320; **FAT** 15G (SAT 6.5G, MONO 5.1G, POLY 1.2G); **PROTEIN** 10G;
CARB 41G; **FIBER** 1G; **CHOL** 90MG; **IRON** 1MG; **SODIUM** 330MG; **CALC** 135MG

Individual Chocolate
CHEESECAKES

PREP: 20 MINUTES   **UNDER PRESSURE:** 8 MINUTES   **TOTAL:** 4 HOURS 59 MINUTES

2 cups water
Cooking spray
¼ cup chocolate wafer crumbs
  (about 5 cookies; such as
  Nabisco Famous Chocolate
  Wafers)
1 ounce bittersweet chocolate,
  chopped
⅓ cup sugar
2 tablespoons Dutch process
  cocoa
1 (8-ounce) block ⅓-less-fat
  cream cheese, softened
½ teaspoon vanilla extract
1 large egg
½ cup fresh raspberries
Frozen whipped topping,
  thawed (optional)

1 Pour 2 cups water into a 6-quart pressure cooker; place a trivet in bottom of cooker.

2 Coat 4 (6-ounce) ramekins or custard cups with cooking spray. Sprinkle 1 tablespoon cookie crumbs in the bottom of each ramekin.

3 Place chocolate in a small microwave-safe bowl. Microwave at HIGH 30 seconds or until chocolate melts; cool.

4 Place sugar, cocoa, and cream cheese in a food processor; process until smooth. Add vanilla, egg, and melted chocolate; process until blended, scraping sides of bowl as needed. Divide chocolate mixture among ramekins. Wrap each ramekin entirely with foil. Place ramekins on trivet in cooker.

5 Close lid securely; bring to high pressure over high heat (about 3 minutes). Adjust heat to medium or level to maintain high pressure; cook 8 minutes. Remove from heat; let stand 6 minutes or until pressure releases. Remove lid.

6 Cool ramekins slightly. Carefully remove ramekins from cooker; place on a wire rack. Blot ramekins with a towel to remove any water that collected on top of foil; remove foil. Cool 30 minutes. Cover with plastic wrap, and chill at least 4 hours. Top with raspberries and, if desired, topping before serving.

SERVES 4 (SERVING SIZE: 1 CHEESECAKE AND 2 TABLESPOONS RASPBERRIES)
CALORIES 310; **FAT** 17G (SAT 9G, MONO 2G, POLY 5G); **PROTEIN** 9G;
CARB 43G; **FIBER** 2G; **CHOL** 90MG; **IRON** 2MG; **SODIUM** 262MG; **CALC** 77MG

COCONUT CRÈME CARAMEL

PREP: 12 MINUTES   **UNDER PRESSURE:** 8 MINUTES   **TOTAL:** 7 HOURS 30 MINUTES

12 MINUTE PREP!

2 cups plus 3 tablespoons water, divided
Cooking spray
1 cup sugar, divided
4 large eggs, lightly beaten
¼ teaspoon salt
2 cups whole milk
1 cup canned light coconut milk
½ cup flaked sweetened coconut, toasted

1 Pour 2 cups water into a 6-quart pressure cooker; place a trivet in bottom of cooker. Lightly coat 8 (6-ounce) custard cups or ramekins with cooking spray. Combine ½ cup sugar and 3 tablespoons water in a small saucepan. Cook over medium-high heat 2 minutes or until sugar dissolves, shaking pan gently as needed to dissolve sugar evenly. Cook 4 minutes or until sugar mixture is light amber (do not stir). Immediately pour sugar mixture into prepared custard cups, tipping cups quickly to coat bottoms of cups.

2 Combine eggs, ½ cup sugar, and salt in a large bowl; stir with a whisk. Add milk and coconut milk, stirring with a whisk. Divide mixture among prepared custard cups. Cover and wrap each custard cup entirely with foil. Place 4 custard cups on trivet in cooker; stack remaining 4 custard cups on top.

3 Close lid securely; bring to high pressure over high heat (about 7 minutes). Adjust heat to medium or level to maintain high pressure; cook 8 minutes. Remove from heat; place cooker under cold running water. Remove lid. Make a small slit in center of custards with a knife (cutting through foil); knife should come out almost clean. If not, replace lid, and return to high pressure; cook 1 to 2 minutes. Remove from heat; place cooker under cold running water. Remove lid.

4 Cool custards slightly. Carefully remove custard cups from cooker; place on a wire rack. Remove foil. Cool 1 hour. Cover surfaces of custards with plastic wrap; chill 6 hours or overnight. Loosen edges of custards with a knife or rubber spatula. Place a dessert plate, upside down, on top of each custard cup; invert custards onto plates, and sprinkle with coconut.

SERVES 8 (SERVING SIZE: 1 CUSTARD AND 1 TABLESPOON COCONUT)
CALORIES 210; **FAT** 8G (SAT 5G, MONO 1.5G, POLY 0.6G); **PROTEIN** 5G;
CARB 32G; **FIBER** 1G; **CHOL** 100MG; **IRON** 1MG; **SODIUM** 150MG; **CALC** 84MG

MOLTEN PEANUT BUTTER CAKES

Powdered peanut butter has the same peanutty taste as traditional peanut butter, but with less fat and fewer calories.

PREP: 19 MINUTES   **UNDER PRESSURE:** 8 MINUTES   **TOTAL:** 27 MINUTES

3 cups plus 3 tablespoons water, divided
Cooking spray
2 tablespoons powdered peanut butter
4 ounces semisweet chocolate, coarsely chopped
¼ cup unsalted butter
1 cup powdered sugar
¹⁄₁₆ teaspoon fine sea salt
2 large eggs, lightly beaten
6 tablespoons all-purpose flour
8 teaspoons frozen whipped topping, thawed
Chocolate shavings (optional)

1 Pour 3 cups water into a 6-quart pressure cooker; place a trivet in bottom of cooker. Coat 4 (8-ounce) ramekins or custard cups with cooking spray; set aside.

2 Combine peanut butter powder and 3 tablespoons water in a small bowl, stirring until smooth. Place chocolate and butter in a large microwave-safe bowl. Microwave at HIGH 1 minute or until chocolate melts, stirring after 30 seconds. Stir in sugar and peanut butter mixture. Cool 5 minutes. Add salt and eggs, stirring with a whisk. Stir in flour.

3 Divide chocolate mixture among prepared ramekins. Cover each ramekin tightly with foil. Place ramekins on trivet in cooker (do not let ramekins touch sides of cooker).

4 Close lid securely; bring to high pressure over high heat (about 4 minutes). Adjust heat to medium or level to maintain high pressure; cook 8 minutes. Remove from heat; place cooker under cold running water. Remove lid. Carefully remove ramekins from cooker; remove foil. Top each cake with whipped topping, and, if desired, chocolate shavings. Serve immediately.

SERVES 8 (SERVING SIZE: ½ CAKE AND 1 TEASPOON WHIPPED TOPPING)
CALORIES 240; **FAT** 13G (SAT 7G, MONO 2G, POLY 0.5G); **PROTEIN** 4G;
CARB 31G; **FIBER** 1G; **CHOL** 63MG; **IRON** 2MG; **SODIUM** 48MG; **CALC** 20MG

PUMPKIN PIE CUSTARDS
with Gingersnap Topping

Be careful not to overcook these custards, as they will continue to cook even after they are removed from the pressure cooker.

PREP: 8 MINUTES UNDER PRESSURE: 15 MINUTES TOTAL: 4 HOURS 23 MINUTES

4 large eggs, lightly beaten
1 cup half-and-half
1 teaspoon vanilla extract
1/4 teaspoon ground cinnamon
1/8 teaspoon salt
1/8 teaspoon ground nutmeg
1/8 teaspoon ground allspice
1 (15-ounce) can unsweetened pumpkin
1 (14-ounce) can fat-free sweetened condensed milk
Cooking spray
2 cups water
1/2 cup frozen reduced-calorie whipped topping, thawed
8 teaspoons crushed gingersnaps

1 Combine first 9 ingredients (through condensed milk) in a large bowl. Pour pumpkin mixture through a fine sieve into a 1-quart glass measure; discard solids. Divide pumpkin mixture among 8 (6-ounce) ramekins coated with cooking spray.

2 Pour 2 cups water into a 6-quart pressure cooker; place a trivet in bottom of cooker. Wrap each ramekin entirely in foil. Place 4 ramekins on rack; stack remaining 4 ramekins on top.

3 Close lid securely; bring to high pressure over high heat (about 4 minutes). Adjust heat to medium or level to maintain high pressure; cook 15 minutes. Remove from heat; place cooker under cold running water. Remove lid. With a knife, make a small slit in pumpkin mixture (cutting through foil) slightly off center to make sure custard is set (knife should come out mostly clean). If not, replace lid, and return to high pressure; cook 2 to 3 minutes. Remove from heat; place cooker under cold running water. Remove lid.

4 Carefully remove ramekins from cooker; place on a wire rack. Blot ramekins with a towel to remove any water that collected on top of foil. Let stand, covered, 10 minutes. Remove foil; cool 30 minutes on wire rack. Cover and chill at least 3 hours. Top each custard with whipped topping and gingersnaps just before serving.

SERVES 8 (SERVING SIZE: 1 CUSTARD, 1 TABLESPOON WHIPPED TOPPING, AND 1 TEASPOON CRUSHED GINGERSNAPS)
CALORIES 270; **FAT** 7G (SAT 3.5G, MONO 2.3G, POLY 0.7G); **PROTEIN** 9G; **CARB** 43G; **FIBER** 2G; **CHOL** 110MG; **IRON** 2MG; **SODIUM** 170MG; **CALC** 192MG

Sticky
TOFFEE PUDDINGS

PREP: 20 MINUTES   **UNDER PRESSURE:** 16 MINUTES   **TOTAL:** 48 MINUTES

2 cups water
Baking spray with flour
¾ cup chopped pitted Medjool dates
½ teaspoon baking soda
1 cup boiling water
6.75 ounces all-purpose flour (about 1½ cups)
1 teaspoon baking powder
½ teaspoon salt
1⅓ cup packed brown sugar, divided
¼ cup butter, softened
2 large eggs
½ teaspoon vanilla extract
¼ cup half-and-half
1 tablespoon butter
½ teaspoon brandy

1 Pour 2 cups water into a 6-quart pressure cooker; place a trivet in bottom of cooker. Coat 8 (6-ounce) ramekins or custard cups with baking spray with flour. Combine dates and baking soda in a medium bowl; add 1 cup boiling water, and stir to combine. Cool 10 minutes.

2 While date mixture cools, weigh or lightly spoon flour into dry measuring cups; level with a knife. Combine flour, baking powder, and salt in a medium bowl, stirring with a whisk. Beat 1 cup brown sugar and ¼ cup butter at medium speed with an electric mixer until light and fluffy. Add eggs, 1 at a time, beating well after each addition. Beat in vanilla. Stir in date mixture. Gently stir in flour mixture, stirring just until combined. Divide mixture among prepared ramekins. Wrap each ramekin entirely with foil. Place 4 ramekins on trivet in cooker; stack remaining 4 ramekins on top.

3 Close lid securely; bring to high pressure over high heat (about 6 minutes). Adjust heat to medium or level to maintain high pressure; cook 16 minutes. Remove from heat; let stand 4 minutes or until pressure releases. Remove lid. Make a small slit in center of puddings with a knife (cutting through foil); knife should come out almost clean. Cool slightly. Carefully remove ramekins from cooker; place on a wire rack. Remove foil. Cool puddings slightly.

4 Combine ⅔ cup brown sugar, half-and-half, and 1 tablespoon butter in a small saucepan. Bring to a boil over medium heat, stirring constantly. Cook 1 to 2 minutes or until slightly thick, stirring occasionally. Add brandy. Remove from heat. Run a knife around edges of puddings. Carefully invert onto plates; top evenly with sauce.

SERVES 8 (SERVING SIZE: 1 PUDDING AND 1 TABLESPOON SAUCE)
CALORIES 325; **FAT** 8G (SAT 5G, MONO 0.3G, POLY 1.5G); **PROTEIN** 4G;
CARB 65G; **FIBER** 1.6G; **CHOL** 66MG; **IRON** 2MG; **SODIUM** 230MG; **CALC** 88MG

NUTRITIONAL INFORMATION

How to Use It and Why

Glance at the end of any *Cooking Light* recipe, and you'll see how committed we are to helping you make the best of today's light cooking. With chefs, registered dietitians, home economists, and a computer system that analyzes every ingredient we use, *Cooking Light* gives you authoritative dietary detail like no other magazine. We go to such lengths so you can see how our recipes fit into your healthful eating plan. If you're trying to lose weight, the calorie and fat figures will probably help most. But if you're keeping a close eye on the sodium, cholesterol, and saturated fat in your diet, we provide those numbers, too. And because many women don't get enough iron or calcium, we can help there, as well. Finally, there's a fiber analysis for those of us who don't get enough roughage.

Here's a helpful guide to put our nutritional analysis numbers into perspective. Remember, one size doesn't fit all, so take your lifestyle, age, and circumstances into consideration when determining your nutrition needs. For example, pregnant or breast-feeding women need more protein, calories, and calcium. And women older than 50 need 1,200mg of calcium daily, 200mg more than the amount recommended for younger women.

In Our Nutritional Analysis, We Use These Abbreviations

sat	saturated fat	CARB	carbohydrates	g	gram
mono	monounsaturated fat	CHOL	cholesterol	mg	milligram
poly	polyunsaturated fat	CALC	calcium		

Daily Nutrition Guide

	Women ages 25 to 50	Women over 50	Men ages 24 to 50	Men over 50
Calories	2,000	2,000 or less	2,700	2,500
Protein	50g	50g or less	63g	60g
Fat	65g or less	65g or less	88g or less	83g or less
Saturated Fat	20g or less	20g or less	27g or less	25g or less
Carbohydrates	304g	304g	410g	375g
Fiber	25g to 35g	25g to 35g	25g to 35g	25g to 35g
Cholesterol	300mg or less	300mg or less	300mg or less	300mg or less
Iron	18mg	8mg	8mg	8mg
Sodium	2,300mg or less	1,500mg or less	2,300mg or less	1,500mg or less
Calcium	1,000mg	1,200mg	1,000mg	1,000mg

The nutritional values used in our calculations either come from The Food Processor, Version 10.4 (ESHA Research), or are provided by food manufacturers.

METRIC EQUIVALENTS

The information in the following charts is provided to help cooks outside the United States successfully use the recipes in this book. All equivalents are approximate.

Cooking/Oven Temperatures

	Fahrenheit	Celsius	Gas Mark
Freeze Water	32° F	0° C	
Room Temp.	68° F	20° C	
Boil Water	212° F	100° C	
Bake	325° F	160° C	3
	350° F	180° C	4
	375° F	190° C	5
	400° F	200° C	6
	425° F	220° C	7
	450° F	230° C	8
Broil			Grill

Liquid Ingredients by Volume

¼ tsp	=					1 ml
½ tsp	=					2 ml
1 tsp	=					5 ml
3 tsp	=	1 Tbsp	=	½ fl oz	=	15 ml
2 Tbsp	=	⅛ cup	=	1 fl oz	=	30 ml
4 Tbsp	=	¼ cup	=	2 fl oz	=	60 ml
5⅓ Tbsp	=	⅓ cup	=	3 fl oz	=	80 ml
8 Tbsp	=	½ cup	=	4 fl oz	=	120 ml
10⅔ Tbsp	=	⅔ cup	=	5 fl oz	=	160 ml
12 Tbsp	=	¾ cup	=	6 fl oz	=	180 ml
16 Tbsp	=	1 cup	=	8 fl oz	=	240 ml
1 pt	=	2 cups	=	16 fl oz	=	480 ml
1 qt	=	4 cups	=	32 fl oz	=	960 ml
				33 fl oz	=	1000 ml = 1 l

Dry Ingredients by Weight

(To convert ounces to grams, multiply the number of ounces by 30.)

1 oz	=	¹⁄₁₆ lb	=	30 g
4 oz	=	¼ lb	=	120 g
8 oz	=	½ lb	=	240 g
12 oz	–	¾ lb	–	360 g
16 oz	=	1 lb	=	480 g

Length

(To convert inches to centimeters, multiply the number of inches by 2.5.)

1 in	=			2.5 cm
6 in	=	½ ft	=	15 cm
12 in	=	1 ft	=	30 cm
36 in	=	3 ft	= 1 yd =	90 cm
40 in	=			100 cm = 1 m

Equivalents for Different Types of Ingredients

Standard Cup	Fine Powder (ex. flour)	Grain (ex. rice)	Granular (ex. sugar)	Liquid Solids (ex. butter)	Liquid (ex. milk)
1	140 g	150 g	190 g	200 g	240 ml
¾	105 g	113 g	143 g	150 g	180 ml
⅔	93 g	100 g	125 g	133 g	160 ml
½	70 g	75 g	95 g	100 g	120 ml
⅓	47 g	50 g	63 g	67 g	80 ml
¼	35 g	38 g	48 g	50 g	60 ml
⅛	18 g	19 g	24 g	25 g	30 ml

INDEX

ISBN-13: 978-0-8487-4349-9
ISBN-10: 0-8487-4349-0
Library of Congress Control Number: 2014959957

Printed in the United States of America
First Printing 2015

Oxmoor House

Editorial Director: Leah McLaughlin
Creative Director: Felicity Keane
Art Director: Christopher Rhoads
Executive Photography Director: Iain Bagwell
Executive Food Director: Grace Parisi
Senior Editors: Andrea C. Kirkland, MS, RD;
    Betty Wong
Managing Editor: Elizabeth Tyler Austin
Assistant Managing Editor: Jeanne de Lathouder

Cooking Light Pressure Cooking Made Simple

Project Editor: Emily Chappell Connolly
Editorial Assistant: April Smitherman
Designer: Maribeth Jones
Assistant Test Kitchen Manager:
    Alyson Moreland Haynes
Recipe Developers and Testers: Stefanie Maloney,
    Callie Nash, Karen Rankin
Food Stylists: Nathan Carrabba, Victoria E. Cox,
    Margaret Monroe Dickey, Catherine Crowell Steele
Photo Editor: Kellie Lindsey

Senior Photographer: Hélène Dujardin
Senior Photo Stylists: Kay E. Clarke,
    Mindi Shapiro Levine
Senior Production Managers: Greg A. Amason,
    Sue Chodakiewicz

Contributors

Recipe Developer: Nancy S. Hughes
Recipe Tester: Tamara Goldis, RD
Writer: Tori Ritchie
Copy Editors: Jacqueline Giovanelli, Dolores Hydock
Proofreader: *Marra*thon Production Services
Indexer: Mary Ann Laurens
Fellows: Laura Arnold, Kylie Dazzo, Nichole Fisher,
    Loren Lorenzo, Anna Ramia, Caroline Smith,
    Amanda Widis
Food Stylist: Erica Hopper
Photographers: Victor Protasio, Becky Stayner,
    Brian Woodcock
Photo Stylists: Cindy Barr, Mary Carl Clayton,
    Missie Crawford
Hand Model: Gardner Park

Time Home Entertainment Inc.

Publisher: Margot Schupf
Vice President, Finance: Vandana Patel
Executive Director, Marketing Services: Carol Pittard
Publishing Director: Megan Pearlman
Assistant General Counsel: Simone Procas